FERRARI

· T · H · E ·

Enduring Legend

Text and photography by

NICKY WRIGHT

FERRARI

· T · H · E ·

Enduring Legend

GALLERY BOOKS
An Imprint of W. H. Smith Publishers Inc.
112 Madison Avenue
New York City 10016

DEDICATION

For Hilary Raab, Jr. and Dave Cummins, whose help I could not have done without. This book is for you. And to Dudley and Sally Mason-Styrron a very special thank you.

ACKNOWLEDGEMENT

The author gratefully acknowledges the invaluable assistance provided by the following individuals and organizations throughout the preparation of this book:

Fuji Films; Pentax Cameras; Milland Place Hotel, Milland, U.K. for their courtesy and help in a location that is traditional Old England; Jack's Camera Shop, Muncie, Indiana; Auburn-Cord-Duesenberg Museum, Auburn, Indiana – Skip Marketti, Lee M.; Modena Engineering Ltd. – Jock Bruce; National Motor Museum, Beaulieu, U.K.; Wayne Nelson; Dennis Machell; Tom Mittler; Wayne Colomb; Hilary Raab, Jr.; Dave Cummins; Mark Tippetts; Dudley and Sally Mason-Styrron; J. Agace Esq; Larry Nicklin; Roy and Barb Hathaway; Donna Begley; Joe Wright and Robert; and Matt Calloway.

Designed by Dick Richardson

Picture captions by Graham Gauld

CLB 2352
©1990 Colour Library Books Ltd., Godalming, Surrey, England.
This edition published in 1990 by Gallery Books,
an imprint of W.H. Smith Publishers, Inc.,
112 Madison Avenue, New York 10016.
Printed and bound in Italy by New Interlitho.
All rights reserved.
ISBN 0 8317 3225 3

Gallery Books are available for bulk purchase for sales preomotions and premium use. For details write or telephone the Manager of Special Sales, W.H. Smith Publishers, Inc.,
112 Madison Avenue, New York, New York 10016. (212) 532-6600

INTRODUCTION

Ever since the first car took to the road over a century ago, man has been fascinated by the automobile. True, many people are equally intrigued by airplanes, ships and trains, though perhaps for reasons a little different from those reserved for the motor-car. One cannot store ocean liners or battleships on a garden pond, and few lawns are big enough to house a B-29 bomber. Unless one owns a large ranch in Texas there is little point in keeping a giant locomotive. That is where the car comes in; it is compact enough to live in its own little establishment alongside the house, and if there is no garage, well, it will make do with the driveway instead.

Besides the logistics involved in owning one or other of the aforementioned, there is also the question of availability. Cars are built for everyone to enjoy, for everyone to buy – hence the millions that pour out of industrialized nations' factories every year. Planes and ships are fare-paying passenger conveyances or tools of war, while trains are somewhat restricted to pre-set routes and to how much track they have. Cars can go almost anywhere on land and are relatively uncomplicated, easy for most people to master and great fun for the millions who enjoy motor racing, rallying, going to car shows, or just waxing the family motor on a sunny afternoon.

Sometimes fascination and enjoyment turns into obsession. While that is perhaps understandable, it can be carried to excess, as in a case, known to the autho,r of the person who talked to his car as others might talk to their flowers. In the case of this enthusiast, his car is a special breed – not the mundane four-door sedan but a car of distinction: a work of art on wheels, almost. In no case can that definition be used more appropriately than of the Ferraris.

Since its debut in 1948, the Ferrari, more than any other make of car, has stirred a million hearts, spun a web of mystique around the designers and engineers, and appeared in a variety of shapes so graceful in style that it would hardly be out of keeping in an art gallery.

No single make of car quite captures man's spirit as does Ferrari. One can talk about the fervor owners have for their Mustangs, MGs, Porsches and Packards, but once the show event is over, the day done and the new trophy admired atop the mantelpiece, then with genuine feelings of love and pride, the Mustang is put away and the owner returns to his family. In most cases, that is; there are exceptions.

With the Ferrari fanatic quite often there is no family life. Ferraris and families are a rare combination indeed. Once ensnared by the Modena mania, there is no turning back – little to be gained from any relationship unless it can match the curves of a Vignale, the rrump! rrump! of a Colombo. The Prancing Horse emblem is the door knocker; the antique mahogany table lies unseen under a coating of Ferrari literature, the drawing-room shelves lined with Ferrari books, the dining-room ones with little Ferrari models. And of course, a photograph of the genius himself looking down through darkened glasses, Enzo Ferrari.

Enzo Ferrari lived his life the way many of his devotées would wish to live theirs. Born in Modena in 1898, young Ferrari caught the mechanical bug from his father, who saw the automobile as the way to a prosperous future.

As a young man, Enzo developed more of an interest in auto racing than in conventional cars. Often he was to be found at the racetrack, marveling at the sights, sounds and smells of the ponderous machines – in those far-off days racing cars were not the aerodynamic wedges of today – they looked a great deal more ungainly round the circuit. Enzo's heroes were racing drivers; this, he decided, was what he wanted to be when he grew up.

At the end of World War I, Enzo Ferrari was discharged from the Italian army after a major operation. Back in civilian life, Enzo pursued his goal to become a racing driver. After one or two false starts and a stint with Costrusioni Meccaniche Nationale, a company that built cars, including racers, from Isotta Fraschini parts, Enzo obtained a job as racing driver for Alfa Romeo.

That was in 1920. Thrown in at the deep end, Enzo found his teammates were the fabled Antonio Ascari and Giuseppe Campari, two of the greatest racing drivers of that time.

It did not take Ferrari long to show his mettle as a driver and, by 1923, he had consolidated his position in Alfa Romeo's racing department. Soon he was spending more time on the design of both sports/racing and passenger cars and less time on the track. His abilities and enthusiasm did not go unnoticed, and it was not long before he was given the post as manager of Alfa's racing program.

Selling cars was a cut-throat business after World War I and anything a manufacturer could do to help sales of his products was eagerly done. By far the greatest effect on sales was competition. Thus many car makers fielded complete racing teams and Alfa Romeo was no exception.

With Ferrari heading its racing team, Alfa went from strength to strength. Men such as engineering genius Vittorio Jano and technician Luigi Bassi left Fiat (which also had its own racing department at the time) to join Ferrari. Then there were established Alfa drivers like Ascari and Campari to take the checkered flag.

With the brilliant Jano-designed Alfa P2 winning numerous races, the Milanese car company won its first World Manufacturer's Championship in 1925, though not before the tragic loss of Ascari when he crashed on the banked Montlhery circuit in July of that year.

Because of a new displacement rule, P2s were banned from Grand Prix racing but continued, from 1926 to 1930, to pile success upon success in other important races, often driven by independent teams who purchased their cars from Alfa.

As time wore on, the young Ferrari became restless, so much so that in 1929 he left Alfa to set up on his own. At the end of the year that saw America on its knees after the infamous Wall Street Crash, Ferrari formed the Societa Anonima Scuderia Ferrari. The idea was to form a racing team composed of skillful amateurs sponsored by enthusiasts and interested corporations.

In its first season, this odd cooperative of amateur drivers financed by firms such as Bosch and Pirelli, rewarded Enzo with nine 1sts, five 2nds and five 3rd places. Still carrying its "amateur" banner, Scuderia entered 1931 full of confidence, and Alfa's new P3 model driven by the legendary Nuvolari, the 2300 Alfa, won the Targa Florio and Italian Grand Prix.

Previous pages: the Ferrari 250 GT Europa with coachwork by Pininfarina – the first Ferrari to use the Gran Turismo title. Powered by a 3-liter V12 engine, it displayed all the hallmarks of what was to become the Ferrari tradition: style, speed and charisma. Facing page: six years and much development later, the 250 GT had become the 250 GT SWB (short wheel base). Designed for competition as well as the road, it developed a reputation that has stayed with it until today and is a much prized collectors' item.

The American depression caused widespread effects in Europe too; companies collapsed and unemployment soared. Alfa Romeo became unable to satisfy its creditors. The Italian Government, considering the firm an important part of the country's industrial structure, put it under state control. Under the new management, racing activities were handed over to Scuderia Ferrari.

From 1933 through 1937 Scuderia Ferrari gave a good account of itself, although its Alfa Romeos were no match for the mighty Mercedes and Auto Unions of the Third Reich. In an effort to close the gap, Ferrari and Luigi Bazzi designed an extraordinary car called the Bi-Motore. Built mostly from Alfa parts, the Bi-Motore deployed one engine in front of the cockpit, another behind it. One car was built for Nuvolari and had two 3.2-liter straights, while the other employed two 2.9 liter, eight-cylinder units.

Both cars were fast and reliable, with the exception of the tires – they could not withstand the enormous power put out by the Bi-Motores and quickly shredded. So instead Ferrari went out to attack a few world speed records. Driven by the indomitable Nuvorali the Bi-Motore set two new Class B international records; the flying kilometer at 199.92 mph and the flying mile at 200.77 mph. So the Bi-Motores' career ended on a triumphant note.

Other cars were developed between Alfa and Scuderia, but they could not equal those fielded by the Germans. When Alfa or Scuderia cars did win, it was due to the Italians' superior driving.

Late in 1937 Alfa Romeo announced it would return to racing the following season. Having been effectively out of it since 1933, Alfa offered Ferrari the position of manager for its racing program. With no cars yet strong enough to do effective battle with the Germans, Ferrari accepted.

Gioachinno Colombo had been a top designer for Alfa Romeo since the 1920s and when Ferrari asked permission to build four 1.5-liter supercharged cars, Alfa sent him Colombo. The result was a superlative design good enough for Alfa Romeo to use to great effect after World War II.

In 1938 Ferrari, disenchanted with Alfa Romeo's way of conducting matters, returned to Modena to relaunch his own business, Auto Avio Construzioni, for the purpose of taking on contract and design work.

Ferrari's next move was to build new cars for the 1940 Mille Miglia. His decision to do this was taken in December 1939, a mere four months before race day. Using mostly Fiat parts, the eight-cylinder, 1.5-liter cars – designated 815 to comply with the engine's type and displacement – would probably have won the race had one car not retired with a broken valve and the other with a broken timing chain. Both cars led the race before retiring, the second one with a lead of 33 minutes over the number-two car. At least this car set the fastest lap record, at 90 mph.

Then World War II overtook Italy and racing ceased for its duration. As for Ferrari, he had to postpone his ambitions for a while and busied himself throughout the war years manufacturing machine tools, most of his work coming from one major dealer. As more contracts came his way, Enzo Ferrari was forced to open a larger factory on the outskirts of a Modena suburb; the Ferrari legend was to have its origins in this factory at Maranello.

Here it was that the first three Ferraris, Type 125 competizione models, were completed in 1947. From then on there was no looking back, and it was not long before Ferrari's cars would be referred to in a manner generally reserved for high art.

Although Enzo was mostly concerned with racing machinery, it was his road cars that really gave him legendary status. This is partly due to the wonderful V12

engines created by Colombo and Lampredi, and partly, perhaps even more so, to the beautiful coachwork created by Vignale, Pinin Farina, Scaglietti, Booro and Zagato. At no time did any of these specialist coach houses do better work than with the beautiful designs they made for Ferrari – perhaps with the exception of Zagato's Aston Martin.

In the 42 years since the first Ferrari, over 250 models have been built. Some are racing cars, some are one-off exercises in design, and some were limited designs, only

half a dozen or so were made. Each model entails a complete story, so much so that it is impossible to include each one of them here; but with the expert assistance of the Ferrari historians Dave Cummins and Hilary Raab, the author has selected 26 which epitomize Ferrari's achievements in the motor industry.

Between 1956 and 1959 a series of long wheelbase 250 GT Ferraris was produced and it was an ideal platform for many of Italy's leading coachbuilders of the day. This 1958 250 GT is a typical example, being a rare Boano-bodied Ellena. Mario Boano was a very special designer who saw the creation of cars such as this as works of art as well as being pinnacles of design engineering. Though at first glance the car may appear simple, its dimensions, curvature and purity make it something special, particularly when it is remembered that it was designed over thirty years ago. As the following models will show, Ferraris often brought out the best in designers ...and occasionally the worst.

THE ROAD TO GREATNESS

For Enzo Ferrari the War years had enabled him to widen his mechanical and business experience and to enter the business of machine-tool manufacturing. In 1945, then, with a modern factory, a 200-man work force and financial security, he returned to his principal interest, the motor-car.

Although 47 years old, the onset of middle-age did not hamper Enzo's desire to return to the racetrack – not as a driver or manager of other companys' cars this time, but as a manufacturer in his own right.

One of the first things Ferrari did was to enlist the aid of Gioacchini Colombo, who was to design a V12 engine for him. Enzo was much taken with the V12 engines which Vittorio Jano had designed for Alfa Romeo before the war. Colombo, who had worked alongside Jano, was happy to develop a V12 of his own design and readily agreed to join Ferrari in this venture.

Piaggio, an aircraft and scooter manufacturing company, employed a brilliant young engineer by the name of Aurelio Lampredi. Lampredi's talents had come to the notice of Ferrari, who hired him to assist Colombo. This arrangement did not last very long and Lampredi left in a disagreement over the conditions of his employment. Ferrari, however, persuaded him to return. Looking over the history of Ferrari since the War, it would appear that he was not the easiest of men to work with, yet those who did, effectively gave him their all. Although Lampredi was persuaded to return (he remained with Ferrari until 1955), the next departure was Colombo's, who left after only two years.

Even if his stay with Ferrari seemed short, Colombo left behind him the main reason for his – and Ferrari's – greatness: the fabulous short-block V12 engine. This engine, along with Lampredi's long-block design that followed shortly after it, was to be the basis for most Ferrari models throughout the 'fifties and 'sixties.

Colombo's first milestone engine had a bore and stroke of 2.16 x 2.06 inches (55 x 52.5 mm), a displacement of 91 ci (1496 cc) and put out 72 bhp at 5,600 rpm. Compression ratio was 8.0:1. It had a single overhead camshaft per cylinder bank, three type 30 or 32 Weber DCF carburetors, and integral with the engine was the five-speed transmission.

This engine first saw duty in the 1947 Type 125 competizione. As its name implies, the car was intended for racing; Enzo was really only interested in the sport of motor racing and he treated his road-going versions with ill-disguised contempt, which was apparent in the often haphazard attention to detail common in those early road cars.

Only three Type 125C Ferraris were built: one as a single-seater, cigar-shaped racing car; the other two featured slab-sided, open-tourer, two-seater bodywork by Touring of Milan. All cars were pressed into competition and, after a couple of false starts, gave a good account of themselves.

A new crankshaft, coupled with an increased bore and stroke (59 x 58 mm), heralded the Type 159 in August 1947. Only two examples were built: one a single-seater, the other a two-seater, competition tourer. But not until 1948 did the first road-going Ferraris make their debut in the form of the Type 166 series. It was the 166 series – or rather the 166 Mille Miglia Barchetta model – that first made the public aware of the import of what was being developed and constructed in the little town of Modena.

Anything new and interesting to emerge during the immediate postwar years was like a ray of sunlight shafting

SPECIFICATIONS
166 Inter

Type	166
Model	Inter
Years made	1948-1950
Chassis range	007S-079S
Number produced	36
Coachbuilders	Touring, Vignale, Ghia, Stabilimenti Farina, Bertone
Body styles	Coupé, Berlinetta, Convertible
Body material	Aluminum
Seating capacity	2 and 2+2
Engine type	V12 60° Colombo
Displacement	1995cc
Bore and stroke	60mm x 58.8mm
Cyl. head	SOHC, single inside plug, finger followers
Ignition	2 distributors
Compression	8.0 to 1
Carburation	1 x 32 DCF
Lubrication	Wet sump
Horsepower	110/115bhp @ 6,000rpm
Chassis/Drivetrain	Engine/gearbox in front
Frame	Tubular steel with elliptical maintubes
Transmission	5 speed
Axle ratio	5.0 to 1 (& others)
Brakes	Hydraulic drum
Wheels	Borrani wire 5.50 x 15
Front suspension	Independent, A-arms, transverse leaf lever shocks
Rear suspension	Live axle, semi elliptic springs and lever shocks
Curb weight	2000lbs (est.)
Wheelbase	2500 and 2420mm
Track front	1250mm
Track rear	1250mm

Previous pages: one of Ferrari's earliest classics, the 166MM Barchetta or "Little Boat," which was shown for the first time at the 1948 Turin Motor Show. The coachwork, then as here in this 1950 version, was by Touring of Milan which, prior to the war, had clothed many Alfa Romeos, including the legendary 2900B. Above: the underscored Touring of Milan badge and the symbol "Superleggera" (super light) at the leading edge of the hood is the signature of a coachbuilding style that was typical of the Italian sports car designers of the 1950s. Facing page top: starkly simple, the painted dashboard and rivetted Nardi woodrim steering wheel on the 166 MM adds to the aggressive posture of the car and underlines its racing ancestry. Facing page bottom: the 166 MM was a 2-liter car with 160 bhp. The V12 engine was produced to celebrate the marque's first of many victories in the Mille Miglia 1,000-mile race round Italy. In creating this model, Touring of Milan were able to blend beautifully crafted bodywork with flowing lines accentuated by a front fender lip which carries right to the rear of the car with perfect symmetry. Underneath, however, it was still a racing car, with stiff suspension and a gearbox that lacked synchromesh on the two lowest of its four gears. Truly a wolf in wolf's clothing.

through the darkness of enforced austerity. All Europe was striving to begin anew, to put the ravages of war behind them. Perhaps those toiling to rebuild their cities dismissed Ferrari Type 166s as unimportant; but to their children, Ferrari would be the stuff from which youthful dreams were made:

In England, at Donnington racetrack, sometime between 1948 and 1950, a small boy hauls himself up to peer over the wall surrounding the track. The wind rushes through his tousled hair as fleet racing cars go roaring by. Face and eyes screwed tight against sun and wind, the little boy marvels at what he sees. His short trousers are covered in dust, his legs scratched and bleeding from the efforts of his climb. It is not everybody who is as fortunate as he, to see top drivers practicing in cars that Dinky Toys do not make ... well, Dinky made some, but not that Ferrari 166 MM. "One day," the little boy promised himself, "I'm going to own that track and the cars and a Ferrari just like the one I saw today..." and he did.

Today Tom Wheatcroft is a successful businessman who made his fortune in property development. He bought Donnington and he owns the Donnington Racing Car Museum, where he houses his Ferraris, including, of course, a Type 166 MM Barchetta. So, with Ferrari's earliest beginnings as a manufacturer in his own right, a seed was sown. With the Type 166 MM Barchetta – a truly attractive car with inspired Touring-of-Milan coachwork, powered by Colombo's magnificent 121 cid (1992 cc) V12 – Enzo Ferrari created for himself an almost fanatical following without realizing it.

Although his small factory has produced some of the greatest road-going sports cars ever seen, Ferrari continued to express a distaste for anything other than pure racing machinery. It rankled with him that he was forced to build road cars to help finance his racing programs in those early years. It seems ironic to us, for memorable as Ferrari's racing feats have been, it was really his road cars that established the legendary status enjoyed by Ferrari today.

One of the reasons Ferrari automobiles command such extremely high prices is the incredibly short production runs each model had in the early days. In fact, the 37 Type 166 road cars – in coupé, Berlinetta and convertible form – was a high number indeed; most models ran to much smaller production figures of six, nine, perhaps a dozen units. Such low figures would be ridiculously low for the likes of Ford certainly, but Ferrari had no intention of competing in the helter-skelter world of mass production and maximum profit. So long as his cars made enough for him to go racing, then Ferrari was satisfied.

Whilst specialist coach builders fell by the wayside in other countries, Italy's industry proliferated after the war. Whether or not one liked what they did and do, Pininfarina, Ghia and Bertone are almost household names, due in most part to the varied and exciting styles created for Ferraris. Take the 166 for instance. Touring, Vignale, Ghia, Stablimenti Bertone and Farina all produced bodies, although Touring's Barchetta styling was far and away the most successful (Barchetta, by the way, means "little boat" in Italian).

Previous page and right: this is one of just three coupés built by Ferrari and, as was the case with the 166 MM, this model was named after Ferrari's success in the 1951 Pan American Road Race, a town to town event across Mexico which called for rugged performance. These coupés, with coachwork by Vignale, displayed various little touches that were to be emphasized more extravagantly by designers with less restraint. One such was the incorporation of vestigial fins on the rear fenders which were to be taken to grotesque lengths by American car manufacturers three or four years later.

SPECIFICATIONS
340 Mexico Sports Racing

4100c, 80 x 68mm, 280 bhp at 6600 rpm, CR 8.5:1, single ohc per bank, single plug per cylinder, coil ignition, 3 DCF3 Webers, 5 speed gearbox integral with engine.

FS Ind double wishbones, transleaf spring
RS Rigid axle, semi elliptic springs
Wheelbase 2600mm
Track Front 1278mm Rear 1250mm

Notes: A special development of four cars only for the **3rd Carrera Panamericana November 1952.** The bodies, three berlinettas and a spyder, were all by Vignale. Chassis numbers are 0222AT, 0224AT and 0226AT for the berlinettas and 0228AT for the spyder. These cars are sometimes referred to as **342 Mexico.**

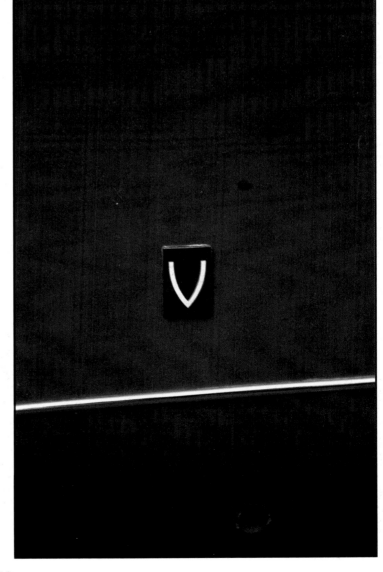

Facing page top: the mighty 4.1-liter V12 engine designed by Aurelio Lampredi differed from the original Colombo engine in that it had a larger block to allow for greater engine capacity. It produced some 280 bhp with a lot of noise and was a racing engine through and through. Above: the front end of the car, styled by a young Giovanni Michelotti, who was to put his mark on many future designs not only for Ferrari but for manufacturers around the world, reflects the by-now Ferrari characteristic of an egg-box grille. Right: though styled by Michelotti, it was during the period when he was employed by Vignale, and the 340 Mexico coupés carried the simple V badge of the famous Turin-based coachbuilders. Facing page bottom: though many enthusiasts might dream of sitting behind the well-used steering wheel of this Ferrari with its simple instrumentation, the car in reality was difficult to drive and had a clutch which did not help the uninitiated to use the gearbox, which had no synchromesh to help with smooth changes.

Powered by Gioacchino Colombo's SOHC V12, an impressive and lasting design, the 166 Barchetta not only looked good but performed well. Displacing 121.7 ci (1995 cc), the engine developed 110 bhp at 6,000 rpm and had an 8.0:1 compression ratio. An unusual feature was a mechanical oil filter that operated each time the clutch was depressed. Top speed was a very respectable 120 mph, and 0-100 was achieved in 27 seconds.

As noted earlier, Colombo's design would be the basis for many of Ferrari's great cars, and by the time it was ready to be phased out, various engineers, such as Alberto Massimino and Vittorio Jano, had honed and improved the unit to perfection. While Colombo's hand was still on the tiller, Ferrari's development genius, Luigi Bazzi, lent a hand to correct any flaws that might have occurred.

Front uspension for the 166 was independent, with double A-arms, lever shock absorbers and a transverse leaf spring. At the rear, the live axle was supported by semi-elliptics and lever shocks. Tubular steel with elliptical maintubes comprised the solid chassis. A five-speed, non-synchromesh transmission was integral with the engine – the fifth gear an overdrive ratio.

Ferraris did well in competition, and it was not long before road-going Type 166s found themselves at the track, where they performed with all the assured ability of their pure racing brothers. All 166s were noisy, even the closed ones – the ride is not for those used to Cadillac comfort – but these were minor shortcomings compared to the exhilaration to be felt driving a machine as powerful as a mythological beast, while being instantly responsive to every flick of the gear lever, every touch of the accelerator, every twitch of the steering wheel. Owners speak of their cars being "alive." It seems to be a part of what the Ferrari fascination is all about. Perhaps they are, if total individuality qualifies them. The body of an early model was hand-formed from aluminum sheets, its engines put together by master craftsmen. Perhaps these men breathed life into the cars, cars which were almost an expression of their personalities. Whatever one may believe, it is an uncanny feeling to be at the wheel of a Ferrari.

In many respects the Type 195 which followed in 1950 was very similar to the 166, the major difference being an increased bore and stroke, which enlarged displacement to 148.3 ci (2431 cc). Brake horsepower was increased to 130 in the Inter, while the 1955 (Sport) went up to 180 bhp at 7,000 rpm.

Only 24 (or was it 28? Opinions vary) 195 Ferraris of both Inter and Sport versions (the Inter had a fractionally longer wheelbase for a reason not fully explained) were built between 1950 and 1952 and, while competition versions did reasonably well, the responsibility for Ferrari's track record fell on the wheelbase of the Type 212.

Displacing 156.3 ci (2562 cc) from the now-familiar Colombo V12, the type 212 entered production during the latter part of 1950. Designated Type 212 Export and 212 Inter GT; the former was the road-racing competition version, the latter for general road use. As with the 195 model, the Inter model had a slightly longer wheelbase. According to the excellent *Ferrari Owners' Club of Great Britain Register* (3rd edition), anomalies occur regarding the precise number of 212 models built. Apparently some normal road-going 212s were labelled "Export" and Ferrari's own impressive records add to the confusion about. Nonetheless, the Ferrari Owners Club of Great Britain estimate that 100-212 models were built between 1950 and 1952 of which about 26 were Export versions.

Whatever the true totals, the Type 212 did well in competition. Export models raced at Le Mans, won the first

SPECIFICATIONS
625 TF

This appears to have been the first of the development cars to have been seen in competition. Not a lot is known about them beyond that they were probably prepared for the **1953 Targa Florio,** hence, it is believed, the suffix **TF** in their designation. They are thought to have been late **166 Mille Miglia Vignale Spyders** fitted with 2.5 litre GP engines. Chassis numbers are listed as 0302TF to 0308TF. Their first competition appearance was at **Monza 28 June 1953,** driven by Mike Hawthorn.

These and previous pages: this car is but one of many mystery cars where the exact provenance is difficult to confirm. Described in the panel above as a 625TF, it was originally described as a 625S when it was tested by Luigi Villoresi at Monza. The model is unique in being the first Ferrari sports car fitted with Aurelio Lampredi's 2.5-liter four-cylinder Grand Prix engine. This beautifully preserved and truly historic car was clothed, as with some of the earlier models, by Vignale. The car was one of three prepared for racing which ran at Monza and Senigallia near Naples. A Vignale-bodied 625TF was also raced at Nurburgring. After they finished racing, one of the cars was converted by Vignale into a Berlinetta and the two spyders were sold to Argentinian enthusiasts Roberto Bonomi and Luis Milan. This is one of the rarest of the early Ferrari sports cars.

Tour de France race and competed in the Tour of Sicily. Ferrari did not win the latter, but by now Enzo Ferrari recognized the importance of the "win on Sunday, sell on Monday" philosophy. His eyes turned to the lucrative North-American market and, more importantly, to Mexico ....

Compared to its wealthy neighbor, Mexico seemed to be from a different time in 1950. Roads were mostly cart tracks, and mules were still used to cross the forbidding mountainous regions. Ideal conditions, thought a group of top-drawer Mexicans, for an exciting road race to end all exciting road races – and so the great *Carrera Panamericana Mexico* or Mexican Road Race, as it was commonly called, came into being.

Even if Mexico was a little behind the times in those days, the wealthy founders of the Panamericana moved with an alacrity not in keeping with the pace of a land of siestas. So good was the planning that the inaugural 1950 race attracted a large number of entries from America to Mexico.

Starting at the Guatemala-Mexico border, the cars battled their way northward to the finish line at Juarez, a distance of 1,320 miles (2,125 kilometers). Most of the entrants drove American cars, but there was a smattering of European vehicles. Considering the forbidding conditions, a surprising 47 cars finished the race, which was won by Hershel McGriff driving an Oldsmobile. Two Cadillacs came in second and third, while fourth place was taken by an Alfa Romeo 6C 2500, driven by the Italian Piero Taruffi – a remarkable achievement considering the Alfa did not have the brawn of its American rivals. Across the sea, in the small Italian town of Maranello, Enzo Ferrari followed the event with great interest....

As soon as Taruffi returned to Italy, Ferrari met him to discuss the race and learn its lessons for the future. In 1951, two Type 212, Vignale-bodied, Export coupés – driven by Piero Taruffi and Alberto Ascari with co-drivers Luigi Chinetti and Luigi Villonesi – were among the entrants for the Carrera Panamericana.

Nobody thought these delicate, finely tuned Italian thoroughbreds would stand a chance against the large, hemi-powered Chryslers or tough Lincolns, let alone survive the course. Ferrari probably had doubts as well, but if he was to crack the lucrative American market, his cars at least had to be fairly high up among the finishers.

Not only did they place well, these two European interlopers surprised everybody, not least the powerful American teams, by winning.

Winning the Panamericana proved a turning point as far as the American market was concerned. Interest spread further even than the enthusiasm of Briggs Cunningham and Phil Hill, the latter raced a 212 Inter in the 1952 Panamericana, and was placed 6th overall.

While the 212 series pushed Ferrari's horizons ever further afield, engineers and designers at the Maranello factory were preparing a remarkable new car for the October 1950 Paris Motor Show. This was the 4.1-liter 340 America.

Previous pages and right: by 1953 Ferraris were in demand by the coachbuilders and were guaranteed show stoppers. This 375 America was an ideal example. Pininfarina in Turin put this low line coupé body on a car which had a racing pedigree – the 375 MM. Whereas the 375 MMs were brutally efficient racers, this street version is one of the most elegant designs of its day. The superbly smooth styling of the rear quarters, with tiny lozenge shaped tail lights and a narrow but swept round rear window treatment, is clear from the picture right. Compared to the racing version which produced 340 bhp. from 4.5 liters, this road car produced 300.

While Gioacchini Colombo's short-block V12 was an excellent design that brought many competition spoils to Ferrari's door – the 1949 Le Mans, the 24-hour Spa race, the 1950 Mille Miglia to name just a few – the engine had its shortcomings. These problems included differential expansion caused by the dimension from the top of the cylinder sleeve to the shoulder which, mated to the block. When the engines ran hot, the compression seal at the copper O-rings was lost.

As noted earlier, these flaws were eventually corrected by the dedicated and inspired team Ferrari had had the good fortune and foresight to gather round him.

Two skilled individuals together in pursuit of the same goal can often result in a clash of temperaments. This certainly was true of Colombo and Lampredi, who disagreed with each other almost from the start. Colombo favored smaller engines which could have a power boost through supercharging, while Lampredi felt it was logical to go for more liters without the corresponding loss of fuel economy inherent in a blown unit. Ferrari, to whom engine technology was sacrosanct, agreed with him, resulting in a much-aggrieved Colombo leaving to rejoin Alfa Romeo. Meanwhile Lampredi, now Ferrari chief design engineer, set to work to prove his point that there really was no substitute for cubic inches.

SPECIFICATIONS
375 America

Type	375
Model	America
Years made	1953-1954
Chassis range	0293AL-0355AL
Number produced	12
Coachbuilders	Pinin Farina, Vignale & Ghia
Body styles	Coupé
Body material	Aluminum & steel
Seating capacity	2
Engine type	V12 60°
Displacement	4523cc
Bore and stroke	84mm x 68mm
Cyl. head	SOHC, single inside plug, finger follower
Ignition	2 distributors
Compression	8.0 to 1
Carburation	3 x 40 DCF
Lubrication	Wet sump
Horsepower	300bhp @ 6300rpm
Chassis/Drivetrain	Engine/gearbox in front
Frame	Tubular steel with oval maintubes
Transmission	4 speed
Axle ratio	Various
Brakes	Hydraulic drum
Wheels	Borrani wire 7.10 x 15
Front suspension	A-arms, transverse leaf springs, lever shocks
Rear suspension	Live axle, semi elliptical springs, lever shocks
Curb weight	2500lbs
Wheelbase	2800mm
Track front	1325mm
Track rear	1320mm

Right: The frontal treatment of the Pininfarina 375 America retained the simple radiator style which had become something of a Ferrari trademark, mated to a symmetrical arrangement of headlights, side lights and fog lights. This particular body is one that is improved by two-tone paintwork, which was less common in those days.

When Lampredi designed his engine he designed it with competition in mind. Road cars were a secondary – though, in financial terms, increasingly important – consideration. So the first cars to get the new engine were a pair of Touring Barchetta Spyders, built for drivers Alberto Ascari and Luigi Villovesi to race in the 1950 Mille Miglia.

This engine was 202.7 cid (3322 cc) and designated 2755. Naturally a V12, the SOHC engine put out 270 bhp at 7,200 rpm and had a bore and stroke of 2.83 x 2.68 inches. It had coil ignition, 3 DCF Weber carburetors and a single plug per cylinder.

Although both cars retired in the Mille Miglia due to tire problems, the engine was satisfactory enough to encourage Lampredi to enlarge its displacement to 250.3 ci (4101 cc). Its first appearance in this guise was the Swiss Grand Prix (it was mainly for Formula One racing that this engine was intended). Its next outing was at Monza, for the Italian GP and although it did not win, Lampredi realized his goal by enlarging it to 4.5 liters. Shortly after that, it won the Spanish Grand Prix, too late to prevent Alfa Romeo taking the championship (Alfa did not even bother to race at Barcelona), but Ferrari's 375 FI 4.5 liter cars gave the complacent Alfa Formula-One team a run for their money in 1951. Alfa won the championship, but only just.

First displayed to critical acclaim at the 1950 Paris Motor Show, the 340 America was the first Ferrari non-Formula One cars to employ Lampredi's long-block engine design. It displaced 250.3 ci (4101 cc) and developed 220 bhp. The show car was a Touring Barchetta, similar in style to the 166 and 212 models that preceded it. Painted black, the displayed 340 boasted a striking green-leather interior not to everyone's taste.

In 1951 a 340 America won the Mille Miglia, the first of many wins for the 340 series; there followed the 340 Mille Miglia and the 340 Mexico in 1952 and 1953 respectively, the latter winning the 1952 Panamericana handsomely.

Only 28 340 Americas were built – 25 if one counts two 275 S cars which were rebuilt with the 4.1-liter engine – of which 16 were street versions. Coachwork was by Touring, Ghia and Vignale, the latter was responsible for the three Berlinetta and one Spyder 340 Mexicos.

Especially built for the Carrera Panamericana, the Type 340 Mexico in its Berlinetta (coupé) form was a handsome and distinctive car, designed by Giovanni Michelotti for Vignale and featuring unusual styling at the front. The front fenders were devoid of headlamps, their rounded peaks ending as two parking lights, while the headlights were set inboard, flanking the familiar oval grille. At the fastback-style rear, the fenders were supplanted by rudimentary fins. Under the hood was the 4.1-liter V12, of course, but with a power boost to 280 horses.

Despite all the preparation for the race, the Spyder did not start and the three Berlinettas were beaten by a 250 MM Berlinetta. All of them survive today, ranking amongst the most desirable Ferraris in the world (two Berlinettas are to be found in America, one in Japan), despite their lack of success in the Mexican race.

Previous pages and right: the Ferrari 250 series was an important landmark as it marked the first use of the Colombo designed 3-liter engine. The 250 Europa was the production version of the racing 250 MM. This particular example was another of Pininfarina's designs similar to the 375 America featured on pages 24-29. As can be seen from this rear view, the rendering of the tail is very similar, but the roof height has been raised presumably to assist rear visibility which must have been limited in the earlier model.

In 1953, Villonesi won the Tour of Sicily with the last of the 340 models, the 340 MM. It developed 300 bhp at 6,600 rpm and is regarded by historians as just a more powerful 340 America. Of the six cars built, two were by Touring, four by Vignale and all were Spyders (open sports).

After the 340s came the 342 series in Ferrari's big-league sports racers. Built in 1952 to replace the 340 street cars, the 342 models shared the same mechanical specifications as their more illustrious brethren. Only one series, the 342 America GT, was realized, of which only six were produced.

Before moving on to the 375 and 410 models, the beginnings of Ferrari's most important series, which spawned some of the greatest sporting cars ever made, are worth discussing. I refer to the 250 series that began with a sport prototype in 1952 and ended with the Lusso (1962-1964). Nobody, not even those who dismiss Ferrari as a "pretender's car," could deny the 250 GTO, 250 SWB Berlinetta and 250 Tour de France are examples of pure artistry. If ever the Italians wanted to recapture some of the spirit of their Roman forefathers, they succeeded beyond measure with their sports cars. Yet Ferrari has never been very innovative, preferring to use techniques already proven by other manufacturers. Somehow all those techniques created a mystique nobody else has yet found out how to achieve.

SPECIFICATIONS
250 Europa

Type	250
Model	Europa
Years made	1953-1954
Chassis range	0301EU-0351EU
Number produced	18/20
Coachbuilders	Pinin Farina & Vignale
Body styles	Coupé
Body material	Aluminum & steel
Seating capacity	2
Engine type	V12 60° Lampredi
Displacement	2963cc
Bore and stroke	68mm x 68mm
Cyl. head	SOHC, single inside plug, roller rockers
Ignition	2 distributors
Compression	8.0 to 1
Carburation	3 x 36 DCF
Lubrication	Wet sump
Horsepower	200/220bhp @ 6,000rpm
Chassis/Drivetrain	Engine/gearbox in front
Frame	Tubular steel with oval maintubes
Transmission	4 speed
Axle ratio	Various
Brakes	Hydraulic drum
Wheels	Borrani wire
Front suspension	Ind., A-arms, transverse leaf springs, Houdaille shocks
Rear suspension	Live axle, semi elliptical springs, Houdaille shocks
Curb weight	Est. 2500/2600lbs
Wheelbase	2800mm
Track front	1325mm
Track rear	1320mm

Right: the magnificent 3-liter Ferrari V12 engine which was much loved by Enzo Ferrari himself. The triple Weber 36 DCF carburetors with their "carrot grater" air cleaners are mounted between the cam boxes in the classic style. The engine was capable of producing over 200 bhp, but it was to be developed for many years to come and can truly be described as one of the classic engines to come from Ferrari.

THE PRANCING HORSE MULTIPLIES

Anyone on the Maranello to Formigine road in the early morning of March 1, 1952, would have witnessed what to them was an apparently unimportant event, but one which in fact had a major influence on Ferrari fortunes. For it was on that road 38 years ago, that a Vignale-bodied Berlinetta Ferrari prototype, fitted with a new 3.0-liter V12 engine, would have been observed traveling at speed. To local followers of Maranello's movements, the car looked innocent enough; nobody knew it was the precursor to the series that would catapult Ferrari into the big league of sports car manufacture, although this was not the reason for the 3-liter engine when it appeared in 1952. In 1952 America and Europe were far removed from one another in terms of power and wealth. The War had been kind to the New World, its population and cities were unscathed by bomb, bullet or shell; only its servicemen could describe the horrors unleashed on Europe. Lend-lease and the Marshall Aid Plan were America's generous contribution to help a ravaged, broken Europe to rebuild for the future. So in 1952 money was scarce, taxes high and gasoline either rationed or very expensive. This led Ferrari to decide to produce two models; one for Europe and one for America.

Initially both cars used the Lampredi long-block engine. In the American version it displaced 275 ci (4523 cc) but was detuned to 180.8 cid (2963 cc) for Europe. The former was the 375 America, the latter the 250 Europa.

Both models were shown at the Paris Salon in October 1953. The 375, which will be reviewed in more detail later, was the largest Ferrari yet built. Interestingly, both models used identical chassis and were clothed in striking Pinin Farina bodywork, which were claimed to have helped to make him one of the world's most influential designers.

After about a dozen 375s and 20 250s had been built, Ferrari dropped the Lampredi engine and returned to Colombo's small-block unit for the 250 series. This had been occasioned by complaints of understeering, nose heaviness and a 110-inch wheelbase, all of which tended to give the car unwieldy handling properties, making it no rival for the nimble Mercedes 300 SL, which the Ferrari might meet in various competition events.

Hence the return of the Colombo engine. It had been doing sterling service on the race-tracks and had powered the 250 Mille Miglia model since 1952. Based on the original 250 prototype mentioned earlier, the 250 MM achieved distinction in the sports-car racing class as well as being extremely attractive to look at. Seventeen Pinin Farina coupés, 13 Vignale Spyders and one Vignale coupé were built for discerning clients who wished to race them. At the 1954 Paris Salon, the second series Europa GT Ferrari was given its world premier.

Sitting on a 102.3-inch wheelbase, the new 250 Europa GT was a vastly improved car, very responsive and a delight to drive. Colombo's short-block V12 displaced 180.2 ci (2953 cc) and developed 220 bhp at 7,000 rpm. Transmission was a 4-speed, all-synchromesh unit and front suspension was independent, with A-arms, coil springs and Houdaille shocks. At the rear, was a live axle, semi-elliptical springs and Houdaille shocks. This was Ferrari's first use of telescopic shock absorbers: previous cars used the old lever-action type.

There is little question, in the opinion of most people, that the most impressive Ferrari body styles were those dating from the early to late 'fifties, and the bodywork of the 250 Europa GT was no exception. Coachwork by Pinin Farina and Vignale, in coupé and Berlinetta forms, graced

It became very clear by the mid 1950s that the American market would be a major outlet for "street" Ferraris, and at the Brussels Motor Show in 1956 the company displayed the 410 Superamerica (these and previous pages) for the first time. It was based on a long wheelbase chassis which suited the designers, and this beautiful Pininfarina Superamerica was typical of the cars produced between 1956 and the end of 1959. Some of the detail work done by Pininfarina displays a marked cultivation of the tastes and styles of American cars of the period. The chromed oval tail light treatment (facing page top) and the chrome sculpting on the hood (top) reflects some of the detail work of General Motors. The cockpit design (right) was new, with indented and angled gauges and fresh air vents and pale leather upholstery. The stop watches are a later addition. On the trunk lid (above), the names of Ferrari and Pininfarina are linked.

This Ferrari 410 differs considerably from the car shown on the previous page, the Ferrari and Pininfarina names having been removed, leaving only the joint flag motif of Ferrari's prancing horse and Pininfarina's stylized "F". The cockpit features a more traditional layout compared to the Superamerica on the previous pages. Overleaf: perhaps the ultimate Superamerica was this Superfast, which was shown at the 1956 Paris Motor Show and was fitted with a 4.9-liter engine. This car had a shorter wheelbase than the earlier Superamericas, but, with its large tail fins, again reflected Pininfarina's fascination with the then-current American styling. It also reverted to the low roof line and had faired in headlights. Almost as an afterthought, a chrome badge proclaiming "Superfast" was added to the rear fender.

the 35 examples produced of this model. These were the days when Pinin Farina designed not only to make a living but also for the pure joy of creating something memorable. As he became more famous his exuberance tailed off; he became a professional. Perhaps, in the final analysis, Vignale always had the edge with his curved designs, so reminiscent of the sensuality and sculpted classicism of a Renaissance nude. Perhaps not quite as pronounced as Zagato's undulant shapes, Vignale's styling nonetheless caught the Italian preoccupation with form better than anyone else at the time.

Naturally the 250 went racing in various guises, its engine powering either Grand Prix or road-competition cars. This was what the engine was designed for, and the cars posed a serious challenge to Jaguar and Mercedes racing teams. Even non-factory Ferrari teams were consistently successful driving the 250 MM, Monza, Tour de France and others, including the magnificent GTO.

Mention of the Monza brings to mind an interesting anomaly. As the 1955 racing season approached, Ferrari decided that the factory-team cars would run with four- and six-cylinder engines. Half way through their development he decided he could not dispense with Colombo's V12 entirely, so a few Monzas (named after the famous Italian race run at the town of Monza) received the larger engine and should not be confused with the four-cylinder 750 Monza cars. The well-known British driver, Mike Hawthorn, coupled with Umberto Maglioli, actually won the Supercorte – maggione GP for Sports Cars (or Monza race to simplify matters) in a four-cylinder 735 Monza experimental model, but a V12 Monza was placed 3rd in the 1955 event. Of the V12 models only four – two Pinin Farina Spyders and two Scaglietti Spyders – were known to have been built. In fact, the Farina-designed Monza shared much in common with the Austin Healey 3000. Or rather, the Austin Healey had obviously plagiarized the Monza which was around several years earlier than the famous British sports car.

After ten years in the business of making production and sports cars and virtually leading the competition, Ferrari "celebrated" with the introduction of the 250 Tour de France, named after the race it won in 1956. This may be confusing but the car that gave Ferrari the race was the long-wheelbase GT 250 built since 1954. It was after winning the gruelling 3,600-mile road race around France's perimeter, that subsequent long-wheelbase Berlinettas were christened Tour de France from 1957 to 1959.

Distinguishing the various Ferraris is complicated, as will be evident from the following paragraphs; but for the Ferrari enthusiast the list of books at the end of the last chapter will be of value.

Previous pages: this 1957 Ferrari 250 GT California Spyder is one of the first produced. Styled by Pininfarina, this car has a body built by the local company Scaglietti of Modena, which was to build many Ferrari bodies in later years. Right: the same car from the rear showing again a simplicity and cleanliness of line in contrast to the Pininfarina Superfast shown on pages 42/43. The California with Pininfarina coachwork was produced from 1958 to 1962 and in that time it utilized three different engines and two different wheelbases. Though earlier road Ferraris had been heavy and difficult to drive, the California changed all that and this series is still rated as one of the most collectable of early Ferraris.

There were four versions of the Tour de France, each series distinguished by its sail-panel louvers – that is the section aft of the doors on each side, also known as the "C pillar". In 1956, ten cars were built and had no louvers. Then came two versions in 1957, the first with 14 louvers decreasing in height as the semi-fastback panel joined with the trunk. Twelve models were built, two by Zagato.

Fourteen examples were built of the second version, the later car being easily recognizable by its radically decreased number of louvers – only three this time. Then 30 cars were built in 1958 with only one louver. The easiest to distinguish is the 1959 version: while it still had a single louver, the front end was quite different. Only 11 were built.

Although still almost 3 liters (the same as the prototype seen that first day of March 1952), the horsepower had climbed to 280 in some competition Tour de France models. It would go higher yet in a legendary model which produced a thrilling 300 bhp at 7,200 rpm: the Testa Rossa Sports racing machine, just the sight of it is a thrill. Even with a line of memorable and distinguished cars to his credit, Enzo Ferrari surpassed himself with the Testa Rossa.

Above and right: the Scaglietti-built California Spyder powered by a 3-liter engine giving it 126 mph performance and all the right noises to go along with it. It differed from the 250 GT Cabriolet which was built during the same period by having a lighter bodywork and closed in headlights (above left). The Californias attracted custom from the stars of the day, including Brigitte Bardot, who shared her car with her husband of the time, the film director Roger Vadim.

SPECIFICATIONS
250GT LWB California

Type	250 GT
Model	LWB California
Years made	1957-1960
Chassis range	0769GT-1715GT
Number produced	49
Coachbuilders	Scaglietti
Body styles	Spyder
Body material	Aluminum & steel
Seating capacity	2
Engine type	V12 60°
Displacement	2953cc
Bore and stroke	73mm x 58.8mm
Cyl. head	SOHC, single inside plug, roller rockers. †
Ignition	2 distributors
Compression	9.1/9.6 to 1
Carburation	3 x 36/40DCL 6
Lubrication	Wet sump
Horsepower	240/250bhp @ 7000rpm
Chassis/Drivetrain	Engine/gearbox in front
Frame	Tubular – maintubes oval
Transmission	4 speed
Axle ratio	Various
Brakes	Hydraulic drums or discs
Wheels	16" Borrani wire
Front suspension	Independent, A-arms, coil springs & shocks*
Rear suspension	Live axle, semi elliptical springs & shocks
Curb weight	2300lbs
Wheelbase	2600mm
Track front	1354mm
Track rear	1349mm

*Telescopic shocks were introduced in 1958 and 1959
†Some outside plug engines fitted

Even though it made its debut on the tenth anniversary since the first true Ferrari was presented to public view, it is very unlikely Ferrari himself thought of the Testa Rossa as an anniversary car. He certainly was not a sentimentalist when it came to winning races, and the reason for the Testa Rossa was to win races: the 1958 World Sports Car Championship to be precise, in which a 3-liter limit was placed on engine capacity. Already a proven race winner, the Colombo 3-liter V12 powered a breathtaking Pinin Farina-designed body, featuring front fenders scooped out behind the wheels; a long, low nose, and a large tear-shaped blister in the center of the hood. At the rear, the fenders kicked up behind the doors and over the wire wheels. In profile, the Testa Rossa recalled the days when pontoon fenders were all the rage, but in this case they were more than a stylish touch. The design was intended to win races and, after a couple of false starts (the 1957 Le Mans for one), Ferrari took the Sports Car Championship. The Testa Rossa – which literally means "redhead," so named because of the stylized red cam-covers used on its engine – proved invincible, even against the combined might of the sports-car world.

Of course, this first Testa Rossa won many hearts, and continues to do so to this day. Of course, it is not to be confused with the car of the same name built in the 'eighties, which – although a fine machine – should not have been called a Testa Rossa. There is only one model of Testa Rossa and it was produced from 1957 to 1959. Current prices of good, original cars run into millions, which is to be deplored. Most people will never have the opportunity of owning one as long as speculators continue to think of such cars as a means to quick profits. One way to stop this manner of dealing would be to boycott the classic car auction circuit, the major culprit for the inflated prices now sadly regarded as the norm.

Just as highly priced unfortunately, and certainly one of the great Ferraris of all time, was the short-wheelbase 250 Berlinetta. It did not start out as this specific design. In 1958 a new type of Ferrari Gran Turismo was prepared, following a suggestion by an American Ferrari distributor. Presumably in deference to the Americans, the car was named the 250 GT Spyder California.

It was designed by Pininfarina (before 1958 the name was Pinin Farina), but was built at Scaglietti's Modena workshop and had quite similar specifications to the successful 250 GT Tour de France (mechanically the new car was identical).

The 49 long-wheelbase California Spyders were made before being succeeded by the short-wheelbase California Spyder in 1960. At the same time, the 250 GT short-wheelbase Berlinetta made its first appearance at the 1959 Paris Salon. The short-wheelbase Berlinetta had a complicated lineage going back to the Tour de France through long-wheelbase 250 GTs, Californias and short-wheelbase Californias. Infuriating as it may be, these complexities are part of the Ferrari mystique and why enthusiasts find the *marque* so fascinating.

Previous pages and right: this Ferrari 250 GT Ellena was one of the early 250 GTs. Unadorned by coachbuilder's badges, it was built by Mario Boano, who had been a stylist with Carrozzeria Ghia but who left the establishment when he felt that the actual business side of coachbuilding interfered with his artistic ideas. He broke away and formed his own company with his son GianPaolo and son-in-law Ezio Ellena, hence the use of the name Ellena. The 250 GT Ellena has a more razor-edged styling and squared off rear than other Ferraris. Around 50 of these coupés were produced.

The reason for the short-wheelbase Berlinetta's existence was two-fold: firstly to meet the increasingly stringent demands of GT racing; secondly to provide enthusiasts with a street car as similar as possible to the racing version. Not everybody was a qualified racer, but many liked the kudos of a car recognizably related to the competition model. In this respect the Berlinetta succeeded admirably.

In the interests of lighter weight the competition GTs were built from aluminum while the street cars had mostly steel bodies. Naturally the road cars had leather seating surfaces, more luxury, engines slightly detuned and softer suspension. None of this detracted from the car which developed 240 bhp, had a slick, fast ratio four-speed gearbox, four-wheel hydraulic disc brakes, traditional Borrani wire wheels and coachwork either by Scaglietti, Pininfarina or Bertone. Top speed? It appears it was not quite the done thing to talk about top speed in those days – rather like Rolls Royce's reluctance to divulge horsepower figures. In polite circles it was "adequate", but declining standards in the final years as the twentieth century finds the macho-oriented driver demanding top speed figures to impress and score points. It is suspected the absolute top speed of the Berlinetta was in excess of 140 mph in street trim.

Above and facing page: the 250 GT Ellena was originally designed by Pininfarina and farmed out to Boano as Pininfarina's facilities were being overstretched. This model, though less well known than others in the 250 GT range, was notable in using ZF steering. With something over 200 bhp it was a fast touring car and fitted into the Gran Turismo style which gave it its name. When Boano moved on he passed over the company to his son-in-law who changed its name to Ellena.

SPECIFICATIONS
250GT Boano/Ellena

Type	250 GT
Model	Boano/Ellena
Years made	1957-1958
Chassis range	0679GT-0887GT
Number produced	50
Coachbuilders	Ellena
Body styles	Coupé -high roof
Body material	Aluminum & steel
Seating capacity	2
Engine type	V12 60° Colombo
Displacement	2953cc
Bore and stroke	73mm x 58.8mm
Cyl. head	SOHC with roller rockers, single inside plug
Ignition	2 distributors
Compression	8.5/8.8 to 1
Carburation	3 x 36DCF
Lubrication	Wet sump
Horsepower	220/240bhp @ 7000rpm
Chassis/Drivetrain	Engine/gearbox in front
Frame	Tubular steel with oval maintubes
Transmission	4 speed all synchromesh with engine
Axle ratio	4.57 to 1 (and others)
Brakes	Hydraulic drum
Wheels	Borrani wire, 6.00 x 16
Front suspension	Independent, A-arms, coil springs & Houdaille shocks
Rear suspension	Live axle, semi elliptical springs & Houdaille shocks
Curb weight	Est. 2800lbs
Wheelbase	2600mm
Track front	1354mm
Track rear	1349mm

1958 FERRARI 250 TESTA ROSSA

SPECIFICATIONS
250 Testa Rossa

Type	250
Model	Testa Rossa
Years made	1958-1961
Chassis range	
Number produced	33
Coachbuilders	
Body styles	
Body material	
Seating capacity	
Engine type	V12 60°/front
Displacement	2953cc/180.2
Bore and stroke	73mm/2.87 x 58.8mm/2.31
Cyl. head	SOHC
Ignition	2 Marelli distributors
Spark plugs per cylinder	1
Compression	9.8 to 1
Carburation	6 Weber 38DCN
Lubrication	
Horsepower	300bhp @ 7200rpm
Chassis/Drivetrain	
Frame	
Clutch	Single dry plate
Transmission	4-speed, all synchromesh, in unit with engine
Axle ratio	
Brakes	Hydraulic, aluminium drums, iron liners
Wheels	Borrani wire, centre lock, knock off
Front suspension	Independent, double wishbone, coil springs
Rear suspension	Live axle, semi-elliptic leaf springs, trailing arms
Curb weight	
Wheelbase	2350/92.5
Track front	1308mm/51.5
Track rear	1300mm/51.2
Top Speed, mph	167
0-100 mph	16 seconds

Between 1960 and 1962 162 SWB Berlinettas were built; quite a production run when compared to the Testa Rossa's thirty-three units; then again it is only fair to point out that the Testa Rossa was, first and foremost, a racing car built for factory and private teams while the Berlinetta served both as a competition and street car.

Sebring, March 1962. All eyes were on drivers Phil Hill and Olivier Gendebien and not without reason. The two drivers were sharing their skills with a newcomer to the racing scene. It was this newcomer that enthralled the crowd. Small wonder considering the car was the striking 250 GTO being given its first public airing. It did quite well, too, coming in second overall and first in the GT class.

If anything, it was the GTO's shape that caught the eye. By Pininfarina, the styling evolved from a 400 SWB Superamerica built for competition, hence the flush, fared in headlights, smooth, integrated lines ending in a true fastback design at the rear. At Ferrari's annual press conference in February 1962 the GTO shown was devoid of the rear spoiler which became a trademark after one was fitted at Sebring.

*Previous pages and right: one of the classic sports racing Ferraris, the Testa Rossa is considered by some to be **the** true classic Ferrari. This model, the 3-liter V12, was announced by Enzo Ferrari at his annual press conference in November 1957 ready for the new 3-liter Sports Car formula in 1958. The unique feature of many of the Testa Rossas was the cutaway pontoon front fenders designed by Fantuzzi in Modena to aid brake cooling.*

With the exception of three 4-liter examples their engines culled from the 400 Superamerica series, all GTOs were powered by Colombo's venerable 180 cid (2953 cc) V12. Six Weber 38 DCN carburetors, dry sump lubrication, a wild camshaft and a five-speed all-synchromesh gearbox to transmit the power, all added up to a claimed 300 bhp at 7,500 rpm. Four-wheel disc brakes provided safe stopping – a very necessary requirement bearing in mind the speeds these cars could attain. Interestingly, the chassis was almost identical to the SWB Berlinetta with only slight variations due to body shape differences. Although the same wheelbase, the GTO was 6.6 inches longer and 3.5 inches lower.

Everyone who has the slightest drop of racing blood in their veins will declare that the finest, most pure form of motor racing was the Gran Turismo class. This included the great races such as Le Mans, Tour de France, Nurburgring and Sebring. The goal was to win, the cars that raced were Ferraris, Jaguars, Aston-Martins and Shelby Cobras. Cars that looked like cars, drivers that were vulnerable and very human, such as Phil Hill, John Surtees, Graham Hill, Roy Salvadori and Carroll Shelby. Not the affected, spoiled contestants of today's tedious, money-oriented motor racing, but men who gave their all to thrill and entertain, who loved the machines they drove so that they became part of them. For the spectators each GT race was an event to be cherished; a "day at the races" accompanied by friends picnic hampers and a bottle of the favorite cognac. It was fun, it was romantic and the spectator was not at a distance from the team or car or driver he followed; he felt an integral part of the race, almost as close to the driver as his team manager.

If ever a Ferrari was invincible, it was the GTO. Here was the epitome of what Gran Turismo was all about. It had everything; the looks, the speed, reliability and romance. GTOs were invincible during 1962 and 1963. It was Carroll Shelby's Cobras, powered by Ford's superb 289 V8, that gave the GTOs serious competition in the 1964 season, yet it was seldom that Ferrari was beaten. Thrilling races resulted between these two adversaries, who held no love for each other yet were sportsmanlike in their show of respect where respect was due. At the end of the 1964 season, Ferrari took the coveted Manufacturers' Championship, pipping Shelby by 84.6 points to 78.3.

At the end of the season Ferrari announced he would build only a few more GTOs because he thought they were too fast and suitable only for the most experienced drivers to handle. Up to that point twenty-five had been built, and good as his word only a further ten cars were completed in 1963.

Ferrari's anxiety regarding the GTO's safety in the hands of all but experienced drivers was borne out in Fitzgerald, Merritt and Thompson's excellent book *Ferrari, the Sports and Gran Turismo Cars*. Richard Merritt describes the GTO as being a docile, even friendly beast up to 4,500 rpm at which point there would be a sudden and violent surge of power that required a concerted effort to keep it under control. Which tells us that even Ferraris have their moments, hemi-powered Road Runner owners should be alert to their potential.

The Ferrari California range was unashamedly produced for the American market on the urging of their U.S. distributor and former factory driver Luigi Chinetti. This model (previous pages and right) is a Series 2 car produced in the latter part of 1958 with slight engine and chassis changes. Twenty-seven Series 2 Californias were produced until a third series was introduced in 1959. The styling is pure Pininfarina, but again the car was built by Scaglietti in Modena.

A further three GTOs were built in 1964 but were quite different bodily if not mechanically. Three others were also built but were actually rebodied first series GTOs brought up to date. Christened the GTO 64, its shape was quite similar to the 250 LM, especially the roof-line, which lost its famous fastback to be replaced by coupé styling with an almost upright rear window recessed between sail panels not unlike the 1968 Dodge Charger. Shorter by 4.3 inches the GTO 64 was also 2.3 inches wider and 2.1 inches lower. Perhaps not as attractive in some quarters as the Series I GTO, it none the less kept the Ferrari standard flying in victory lane. After the end of the season there would be no more GTOs, the Commendatore preferring to investigate racing life with a new formula, the rear-engined configuration that was the 250 LM.

Up front, where most people consider the engine should belong, Ferrari was not just Testa Rossa, Tour de France and GTOs. These were assuredly the cars that cemented Ferrari into legend, but there were other spectacular 250 models as well. Between 1956 and 1958 in the Gran Turismo series there were the Boano and Boano/Ellena 250 GTs, the former a low-roof coupé, the latter a high-roof version. Chassis and wheelbase were as the Tour de France but they were designed as production road cars.

Shown at Geneva in March 1956, the first Boano was actually designed and built by Pinin Farina, who was largely responsible for all Ferrari's coachwork.

Several prototypes were built by Pinin Farina (about six in all) and the final version was handed over to coachbuilder Boano for series production. Carrozzeria Boano was established in 1954 by Mario Boano who, after building between seventy and eighty cars during 1956 and 1957, joined Fiat to head a new design studio. The Boano coachbuilding shop was taken over by Boano's partner, Luciano Pollo and his son-in-law, Ezio Ellena. A further fifty cars were built by the new team but only a few of them carried the Ellena badge. Oddly, only a very few of the original Boano cars had Boano's shield; whether this was something to do with design copyrights because the car was originally styled by Pinin Farina is uncertain; this could be the case, however.

Then came the Pininfarina (now a single word) 250 GT coupé of 1958. It lasted two years and represented Ferrari production in high gear. Three hundred and fifty examples were built; if that appears a lot, Chevrolet can put it into perspective. While Pininfarina built 350 between June 1958 and the end of 1960, Chevrolet poured out approximately 3.5 million automobiles! This goes some way to explaining why Ferraris fetch such huge prices and are so desirable, yesterday, today and tomorrow.

Nevertheless, 350 units was a lot for a small car company originally formed to build racing cars and forced to produce street machines to pay the bills. Up until 1958 only 800 Ferraris of all types had been manufactured so the number of Pininfarina coupés built represented quite a revolution for the Maranello company.

Right: Some of the details of the Scaglietti Spyder California. The interior featured a relatively standard display with the various temperature and pressure gauges lined up along the dash. It is easy to see how this car brought many converts to Ferrari and its elegance and style was marketed to the full. Even today it looks as modern as the day it was conceived.

1959 FERRARI 250 GT

During the mid to late 'fifties, Pininfarina was obviously quite taken with American design, as can be seen by some of his 410 Superamerica models. If one compares Ford's 1956-1957 Lincoln Continental Mark II with Pininfarina's 1958-1960 250 GT coupé, the windshield, roof and rear pillar are pure Mark II. Even the coupé's long hood suggests Lincoln, but the nose ahead of the headlights and fender line was very definitely a Ferrari trademark.

Appearing in the same year as the 250 GT was the desirable 250 GT California Spyder. Although the design has been credited to Pininfarina, Scaglietti actually built the forty-six long-wheelbase examples between December 1957 and February 1960 and a further fifty-five short-wheelbase units from 1960 to 1963. In all probability, Pininfarina's shop was working to capacity to build the 250 GT coupé as well as the 250 GT Series I and Series II convertibles. Forty-one of the Series I were built between 1957 and 1959 when the Series II took over; 200 left Pininfarina's factory before production stopped in 1962.

By the late 'fifties Enzo Ferrari had come to accept, albeit grudgingly, that the smoothest passage to the race-track was through the sales of his road cars. Relations between Ferrari and Pininfarina could not have been better and both sides made the most of it. People the world over could not get enough of the road-going cars, thus encouraging a steady profusion of models mostly designed and built by Pininfarina. A good example was the October 1960 Paris Salon when Ferrari displayed the California Spyder SWB, a new 2+2 250 GTE and a Cabriolet.

The new 2+2 GTE followed on the heels of the 250 GT coupé, which ended production in 1960. Devising a four-passenger model seemed the logical way to go if help was needed to bring more buyers into the Ferrari camp; although space for rear passengers might have been construed as negligible because the car used the same 102.4-inch wheelbase as the coupé. Power was 235 bhp at 7,000 rpm from the familiar Colombo 60-degree V12, but brakes were discs all round, following Ferrari practice since 1959.

Obviously the right formula for those hungering to own a Ferrari, the rear seats, useless as they were, provided the psychological boost which netted the GTE a production record of 950 units built from 1960 to 1963.

As a saleable commodity to help Ferrari chase world racing championships, the GTE 2+2 was a resounding success. As a styling exercise, it left much to be desired, in this writer's opinion. Slab sides, an odd roof-line which featured a too-large rear window and a C-pillar that tucked in on itself, led to a car more in keeping with the products of the British Motor Corporation (British Leyland after 1967) than with Ferrari. Which is hardly surprising, considering Pininfarina styled a number of BMC models. Much better was the car that joined the GTE in 1962. Not as perfect of line as some Ferraristis seem to believe, but the 250 GT Berlinetta Lusso was an attractive car, none the less.

Lusso means luxury or deluxe, which is exactly what this model set out to be. Built on the short 94.5-inch wheelbase the Lusso was again designed by Pininfarina but the all-steel body (only doors, hood and trunklid were aluminum) was put together by Scaglietti. Interestingly, the Lusso nomenclature was not inspired by the factory, who chose to refer to the car simply as a 250 GT Berlinetta. That Lusso, which was originally used to describe the model, became the car's name, was probably to celebrate Ferrari's first truly luxurious model. Luxurious by Ferrari standards, but certainly not as fully equipped as an Aston Martin or Chevrolet Corvette.

Standard Lusso equipment included well-designed, leather-covered bucket seats which provided good lateral support even if forward and backward adjustments were strangely overlooked.

A thermostatically operated radiator fan was fitted bearing in mind American complaints of overheating in some of the hotter states, and a manually operated radiator blind was included to encourage a higher water temperature in the winter. This enabled the heater and defroster to work when they were needed.

Three hundred and fifty Lussos were built between 1962 and 1964 and ran parallel to the legendary GTO described earlier. Both cars shared the same 180.2 cid V12, though the Lusso, at 240 bhp was 40 horses lighter than the GTO. But it is the GTO, with its appreciably smaller production run, its sporting history and its beautiful design, that commands prices in excess of $2 million today. This does not mean the Lusso is any the less desirable. There are more of them but the Lusso is important because it was the first serious attempt at luxury and it was the last under-3.0-liter road car Ferrari built.

Another Ferrari commanding excessively high prices is the very interesting and unique 250 LM Prototype/GT. It was essentially a closed version of the 250 P sports racer of which four prototypes were built to compete at the 12-hour Sebring, in March 1963. This was a rear-engined car powered by Colombo's V12, a configuration handed on to the 250 LM Berlinetta announced later in the year.

The rear-engined cars were quite a departure for Ferrari and, as such, created much excitement amongst the marque's loyal followers. Named after Le Mans, the LM was supposed to be Ferrari's 1964 challenge to Ford, who had gone racing in a big way, and Carroll Shelby's Cobras, whose electrifying performance came close to wresting the honors from Maranello. Unfortunately it did not quite work out that way.

To enable the 250 LM to compete in the championships Ferrari needed the Commission Sportive Internationale's (CSI) rubber stamp of approval for homologation. Due to a mix up the necessary forms arrived after the April deadline and the request was turned down. In July the ratification committee met again to consider Ferrari's request but turned the LM down as hardly any of the 100 units required for homologation had been built. If the LM could not be used, the GTO could, keeping Ferrari's name aloft the entire 1963 season. As we learned earlier, Ferrari had the Cobras to contend with but amassed just enough points to beat them.

A racing season is a long time in motor sport, so by the time Ferrari made its bid to have the LM homologated in 1964, the car had been honed and refined to near

Previous pages: between 1958 and 1960 yet another Spyder was produced, again designed by Pininfarina. The company had had to farm out the building of their designs while their new manufacturing facility was being built at Grugliasco, outside Turin, but now they were planning the next moves. The Ellena and California were in production, and with the 250 GT they experimented with a lower waistline, which gave the car a long, lithe look. The front grille was lowered and the fog lights mounted behind a chromed egg-crate grille. This model in closed coupé and spyder form became the largest production Ferrari up to that time, and in the three-year lifespan of the model some 350 were produced. The Pininfarina style is immediately visible in the cockpit (facing page top), with the layout of the instruments further emphasised by being raised proud from the dashboard. The headlights were unshrouded and the tail lights similar to a pattern that had been established some time before.

1963 FERRARI 250 GT LUSSO

1955, the 500 Mondial's last year. Some thirty-two examples were built, mostly with Scaglietti Spyder bodies, but three or four Series I cars were Pinin Farina Spyders.

While the Mondial was holding its own, Ferrari introduced a new four-cylinder competition car at Monza on 27 June 1954. Again a Lampredi design, the new 3-liter engine displaced 182.6 cid (2992 cc) and developed 260 bhp at 6,000 rpm. Cylinder head, block, crankcase and sump were all aluminum-alloy castings with cast-iron cylinder liners screwed into the head.

Bodywork for the 750 Monza (as the model was named) was actually draughted by Ferrari's son, Dino. Its lines were clean and reasonably well executed, bearing faint comparison with the 250 Testa Rossa that was yet to come, yet there is an awkwardness of line difficult to explain especially when viewed from above or the side. Whatever its looks, the 750 Monza was probably Ferrari's most successful and reliable four-cylinder car and certainly better than the enlarged 3.5 liter 850 Monza that followed it for a short run in 1955. Only seven 850s were built and its first race was the Tourist Trophy in September – which it did not win!

Other four-cylinder models included the 500 Testa Rossa and 500 TRC. Not to be confused with the legendary V12-engined 250 Testa Rossa, the 500 TR was first shown at the New York show on 28 April 1956. Mechanically the car was similar to the 500 Mondial, and the TRC (introduced later in the year to conform to FIA's Appendix C ruling for 1957, hence the car's new designation), used exactly the same mechanicals even if the car was three inches lower. The bodies, incidentally, were Scagliettis. Fifteen TRs, and twenty TRCs were built before Ferrari ended four-cylinder racing. An interesting sideline was the Ferrari Le Mans entry in 1956. Three TR bodies were equipped with the 2.5 liter GP engine and sent out as prototypes to do battle with Jaguars and Astons. Although the Ferraris, designated 625 LM, could not match the stronger, more powerful British cars, one of the little Ferraris managed to come in 3rd overall behind the first-place Jaguar and second finisher, Aston.

Before a look at Ferrari's first six-cylinder cars, a final note on Maranello's four-cylinder adventures. No road version of the four-cylinder engine had been contemplated until 1961 when a pretty coupé with a Bertone body was shown at Turin.

Underneath the coupé's hood was a 51.9 cid (850 cc) engine. This was Ferrari's half-hearted attempt at marketing an economical baby car bearing his name. This never happened because a good friend of Ferrari, Dr de Nora, bought the complete design outright and put his son, Niccolo de Nora, to work producing the car.

Between 1962 and 1967 about 120 coupés and twenty Spyders were built. The fiberglass bodies were by Touring and Corbetta. Engine capacity was raised to 62.9 cid and the car was a mere 152.8 inches long, on an 86.5-inch wheelbase. That the venture came to nothing was probably due to lack of interest on Ferrari's part and little incentive on the producer's account.

Previous pages and right: the steel-bodied 250 Berlinetta Lusso carried forward the style of the SWB, but rather than being a racing car it was designed purely as a road car and towards that end the engine was moved forward in the chassis to give more room in the cockpit even though it was still designed for just two people. Its impact is best summed up by General Motors stylist Chuck Jordan's remark "The Ferrari Berlinetta Lusso is an excellent example of timeless design." This was one of the finest examples of Pininfarina design. The model was in production for just two years and so only 350 were built, but Jordan's comment about timeless design is appropriate, as it could still command attention today.

1962 FERRARI GTO

While Ferrari was busying himself with fours and V12s in 1955 he decided to compete against the Teutonic power that was Mercedes. To do this he needed a six-cylinder engine to give himself a competitive edge. Already proven and running, Lampredi's four-cylinder engines were an excellent basis on which to build. Instead of starting afresh the engineers simply added two extra cylinders to the four and the first Ferrari in-line six-cylinder sports racing car was the 118 LM (Le Mans).

Only four or five examples of the 118 LM were produced. It used the 2.5 liter four with two extra cylinders added, and while the bore and stroke remained the same 3.70 x 3.54 inches as before, displacement increased to 228.7 ci (3747 cc).

Shortly after driver Piero Taruffi won the Tour of Sicily with the 118 LM, Ferrari brought out the 121 LM. This car had a larger six-cylinder engine displacing 269.2 ci (4412 cc). Based on the 3.0 liter Monza four, this car was a problem child. Although it was clocked doing a fast 175.6 mph down the Mulsanne Straight at the practice for the 1955 Le Mans, the 121 LM was notable for its unreliability. So too was the smaller 118 LM; in their short spell at the race tracks the only race they won was the Tour of Sicily mentioned above. Ferrari abandoned in-line sixes after only four 121 LMs had been built.

While much time was being spent on improving the fours and later, the unsuccessful in-line six, Lampredi's V12 was a masterpiece of engineering. It had already shown its versatility in both sports and GP racing, where it enabled Ferrari to trounce the opposition on numerous occasions.

As has been noted, the V12 was a versatile piece of machinery from which a great deal more power could be extracted. By 1953, after having shown at the New York International Show a 342 America fitted with a 4.5 liter V12, Ferrari introduced the 375 MM. This was a sports racer and its first outing was at Le Mans where, driven by Ascari and Villonesi, it set the race lap record. From such auspicious beginnings it is a shame the car did not continue in the same vein; it retired with terminal clutch problems shortly afterwards.

This car displaced 274.2 ci (4494 cc) and developed well over 300 bhp. It was built over two years, mostly by Pinin Farina although Vignale got his oar in with a Spyder or two. Actually the factory team cars consisted of three Pinin Farina Berlinettas and one Vignale Spyder. Road versions of this model had a larger displacement at 275.8 (4522 cc) ci and developed a huge 340 bhp.

No one is very precise as to how many 375 MMs were built: some say a dozen, others eighteen. One total reads twenty-six, yet another only ten. Hilary Raab, well known in Ferraristi circles as a leading Ferrari historian, lists twenty-eight 375 MMs by serial number in the second volume of his excellent and painstakingly researched books *Ferrari Serial Numbers*. Knowing Hilary well, the author would vouch for the accuracy of his listing over all others, including Ferrari, whose record keeping was farcical at the best of times.

Previous pages and right: the early 1960s were probably the most successful years for Ferrari as they produced a whole series of cars which became classics. The SWB 250 GT had hardly completed its short but successful racing career when along came the Ferrari GTO. What made it special can be seen from the beautifully sculpted lines, which give it the appearance of racing as it stands still. The GTO name came from Gran Turismo Omologato. At the time, for a car to race in the GT class it had to be approved or "homologated" by the racing authorities. What it meant was that a manufacturer could produce an interim design and have it homologated without having to build the usual minimum number of examples.

Some of the aerodynamic elements of the GTO can be seen in this group of photographs. With the 250 GT SWB the racing drivers had complained about aerodynamic lift and this model was put in the hands of Engineer Bizzarrini so that some practical tests could be carried out. The result was a car with a low frontal profile and a tail with a lip to convert air pressure into rear down force. It is this tail feature which stands out in the design of the GTO. Even the ducting behind the rear wheels (facing page bottom) to suck hot air from the brakes was designed for optimum aerodynamics, and the quick-lock gas filler cap was sunk down into the tail section to minimize drag. The car was designed in the wind tunnel of the University of Pisa rather than being just the flight of fancy of an artistic coachbuilder.

After the 375 MM came the 375 America and 375 Plus. Thirteen Americas were built, eight of them were stylish Pinin Farina coupés and other coachbuilders such as Vignale and Ghia made up the rest.

For 1954 Ferrari decided to increase the power of the 375 engine to 299 ci (4954 cc) by combining the 274.2 cid "civilian" engines' 3.30-inch bore with the factory racing units 2.93 inch stroke. Six team cars were built with the enlarged engine and designated 375 Plus. Spyder bodywork was by Pinin Farina, the cars had a new chassis with frame rails that ran over the top of the back axle. As for the improved engine, it developed 330 bhp at 6,000 rpm. Like so many Ferraris, the 375 Plus was around only for a very short time; even so it competed very successfully, winning such trials as the 1954 Carrera Panamerican, beating all comers at Silverstone and doing well at Le Mans.

After the 375 cars came what should be regarded as Lampredi's finest hour (though he was not around to appreciate it, having left Ferrari in 1955). At the end of 1956 visitors to the Ferrari stand at the Brussels Motor Show were greeted with what looked like a stretched 250 Europa. Rather it was Ferrari's first of a superlative new series of road cars, the 410 Superamerica.

Powered by 5-liters-worth of Lampredi V12 (302.8 cid; 4962 cc) which developed 340 bhp at 6,000 rpm, the 410 came in three distinct series totalling thirty-five cars. The first series, built in 1956, consisted of seventeen cars. In 1957 a mere handful (six in all) of the Series II Superamerica were built. This car differed inasmuch as it had a shorter wheelbase, as did the 1958/1959 Series III model (102.4 inches as compared to the long-wheelbase version measuring 110.2 inches).

For the coachbuilders Pinin Farina, Ghia, Boano and Scaglietti the 410 series proved a popular success and provided them with ample opportunities for exercising their stylistic flair. Each car was built to special order and customers included such figures of notoriety and fame as the Shah of Iran, the President of Venezuela and the exiled Emperor of Thailand, who drove his car about Paris rather than Bangkok – which might have been a little risky at the time. Whatever differences there might have been, one thing was certain: all these buyers shared an appreciation for a mechanical and stylistic jewel such as the Superamerica.

It was not that the customers had much influence in deciding how the cars would look; the designers had free rein to devedop whatever interpretation they felt suited the times.

In the mid-fifties it was American automotive styling that had the most influence and this was certainly reflected in some of the more radical 410 Superamerica models. Fins were the "in thing" on the American side of the Atlantic, and while many Europeans deplored the Americans' predilection with fins and chrome, the Italian stylists took to the fad with enthusiasm.

Pinin Farina styled the controversial first Superamerica shown at the 1956 Paris Salon. This was indeed a very special styling exercise featuring a cantilevered roof and a wrap-round front windshield á la Lincoln Continental Mark II, but with no windshield posts! Canted fins made up the rear of this exotic creation but before the car went to its first owner, windshield pillars were added. Many Ferraristis shunned this car at the time, but it has since become recognized as a truly great *tour de force* in the world of art on wheels.

Far wilder and really not at all attractive was the Superamerica designed by Carrozzia Ghia. Borrowing heavily on an in-house styling exercise by Ing. Savonuzzi for

SPECIFICATIONS
250 GTO (berlinetta)

Type	250 GTO
Model	Berlinetta
Years made	1962-1964
Chassis range	
Number produced	39
Coachbuilders	
Body styles	
Body material	
Seating capacity	
Engine type	V12 60°/front
Displacement	2953cc/180.2
Bore and stroke	73/2.87mm x 58.8mm
Cyl. head	SOHC
Ignition	Single distributor
Clutch	Single dry, plate
Compression	9.8 to 1
Carburation	6 Weber 36DCN
Lubrication	
Horsepower	280bhp @ 7500rpm
Chassis/Drivetrain	
Frame	
Spark plugs per cylinder	1
Transmission	5-speed w/reverse; synchromesh, in unit with engine
Axle ratio	
Brakes	Hydraulic discs
Wheels	Borrani wire, centre lock, knock off
Front suspension	Independent, double wishbones, coil springs
Rear suspension	Live axle, semi-elliptic leaf springs, trailing arms
Curb weight	
Wheelbase	2600/102.4
Track front	1354mm/53.3
Track rear	1349mm/53.1
Top Speed, mph	176
0-100 mph	14.1 seconds

Though the 250 GTO used the same chassis as the SWB 250 GT, the whole shape and style of the car changed. The racing rules of the day underlined that in order to be classed as a production GT car 100 had to be built. In the end only 39 were constructed, but by retaining a live rear axle rather than changing the car to independent rear suspension Ferrari were able to indicate that the GTO was merely a development of the 250 SWB, of which many more than 100 had been built. Not for the last time Enzo Ferrari had played the rules and won. On the race track the car was almost unbeatable and gave Ferrari their Manufacturers' Championship. What gave it the edge was the time spent in the wind tunnel improving the aerodynamics and the handling. Most of the 250 GTOs built used 3-liter V12 engines, but a handful of the later models used the 4-liter engine from the 400 Superamerica. The car illustrated on pages 80-85 is one of these and is easily identified by the pronounced high hump on the bonnet compared with the the regular 3-liter car illustrated on the previous and facing pages.

a special Chrysler show car called the Gilda, the 410 was conspicuous for its rear, which was even a parody of Chrysler's finniest excesses.

While the cars this particular Ferrari tried to emulate were handsome examples of art on wheels, Ghia took various elements of American design and succeeded in making them utterly tasteless when applied to the Superamerica. An interesting anomaly was the engine, which was supposedly built as a special order variation for the original owner of the car. Called the 510, Lampredi's V12 grew to over 6 liters and was the one and only time it was enlarged to this size.

With its 6-liter engine this car must have had prodigious acceleration and top speed, but although other bizarre 410s were built, none quite matched this for sheer awfulness! Anyone who knows his Ferraris will agree that Lampredi-engined cars such as 375s or 410s were extremely fast. Certainly the 410, with its 340 bhp engine, could hold its own against Chrysler's amazing 300B, possessing 354 ci of hemi-V8 putting out exactly the same horsepower as the 410. Both cars held the distinction of having the largest production engines in the world and both were the first examples of their breed.

With Lampredi's departure at the latter part of 1955, brought about by disagreements and quarrels with Enzo Ferrari, an era of superlative engine development abruptly ended. The 410 series was the last of the Lampredi-powered Ferraris. His legacy has become part of motoring folklore, his engine types prodigious. Of the 12-cylinder models he was responsible for the 250 Nautico, all 340 models, the 342 and all 375 and 410 models. Then there were the two six-cylinder cars, the 118 LM and 121 LM. As for four-cylinder cars, Lampredi was responsible for a number of them, including the 500 Mondial, Testa Rossa and TRC, all 625s, the 735 Sport, all 750 models, the 857 Sport and finally the 860 Spyder.

It is difficult to say which were Lampredi's best, but if one were to take the 340 Mexico, 375 MM and 410 Superamerica Series I, that would sum up Lampredi's contribution to engine development – in effect his own crown jewels that today would fetch the sort of money one would expect to pay for the British Crown jewels. We are talking of millions for cars whose worth their creators never dreamt would equal that of a Gauguin painting.

At the Brussels Motorshow in 1960, Ferrari unveiled the successor to the 410. This was the 400 Superamerica GT powered by an enlarged 242.1 ci (3967 cc) V12 that owed its origins to Gioacchini Colombo. Lasting four years, the 400 Superamerica stretched over two series. The first was built on a short wheelbase, mostly by Pininfarina. In 1962 the second series appeared, mostly on the longer wheelbase once used as the short one for the 410 series.

All in all, sixty-eight 400 Superfasts were built between 1960 and 1964. The first series consisted of twenty-three examples, lasting until 1962. Forty-five second series cars were produced including a Series III and IV show car.

A new 302.9 cid (4963 cc) V12 heralded the 500 Superfast first shown at the prestigious Geneva Salon in 1964. This engine again owed something to Colombo even if the larger bore centers were an echo of Lampredi. Thirty-

Previous pages and right: one of the last of the 250 GT Berlinetta Lussos. Looking at this car it is hard to imagine that the design is over 25 years old. It was a true classic from Pininfarina. Although not a blindingly fast car as it was purely a street model, it nevertheless had good low down acceleration, which added to the feel and mystique of the car. It would reach 60 mph. in 8 seconds and yet gave a fuel consumption of around 15 mpg. The 250 GT Berlinetta Lusso was the last of the 250 series which had begun nearly ten years before.

SPECIFICATIONS
250GT Berlinetta Lusso

Type	250
Model	GT/L Lusso
Years made	1962-1964
Chassis range	3849-5955
Number produced	350
Coachbuilders	Pinin Farina & Scaglietti
Body styles	Berlinetta
Body material	Steel
Seating capacity	2
Engine type	V12 60° Colombo
Displacement	2953cc
Bore and stroke	73mm x 58.8mm
Cyl. head	SOHC, single outside plug, roller rockers
Ignition	2 distributors
Compression	9.2 to 1
Carburation	3 x 36DCS
Lubrication	Wet sump
Horsepower	240bhp @ 7500rpm
Chassis/Drivetrain	Engine/gearbox in front
Frame	Tubular – maintubes oval
Transmission	4 speed
Axle ratio	4.0 to 1 and others
Brakes	Hydraulic discs
Wheels	15" Borrani wire
Front suspension	Independent, A-arms, coil springs, telescopic shocks
Rear suspension	Live axle, semi elliptical springs, telescopic shocks, Watts linkage
Curb weight	2700lbs
Wheelbase	2400mm
Track front	1395mm
Track rear	1387mm

seven 500 Superfasts in Series I and II were produced over two years by Pininfarina, who designed the one body style. As exotic cars go, it did not have the styling panache of the 410 Superamericas, but with a claimed 400 bhp under the hood its acceleration and speed made up for the not so exciting body design.

Until the 5.0 liter flat 12 of the late seventies and early eighties, the 500 Superfast was the last large-engined Ferrari road car. No V12 went beyond 4.4 liters after the 500. By the time production ended in 1966, mid- or rear-engined cars were much in evidence. In fact, Ferrari stopped using front-engined racing cars after 1961. The advent of the flat-12 engine in 1972 signaled the end of the Modena-inspired productions, their indefinable mystique having reached its peak. Ferrari had matured; it had become professional; it made big money; in substance it had become like everyone else.

Yet some great cars were still to come. The next chapter will describe some of them, including one of the prettiest in the last twenty years, the little Dino 246 GT. The cheapest Ferrari ever produced, the Dino had a transverse, rear-mounted V6 for power and was built by Fiat.

From every angle the Berlinetta Lusso had class. Even the sculpted overriders were shaped to hold the sidelights (above left) while the rear view (facing page top) emphasized the flattened tail which was to become a style feature of many cars to follow. In addition to the normal Pininfarina badge, the company now used the long rectangular badging emphasizing the company's new name Pininfarina rather than its previous name Pinin Farina.

FROM DINO TO F-40 AND SKYHIGH INFLATION

But before the Dino there came numerous other models. In a book of this nature it is impossible to describe the more than 250 types of Ferrari built since 1948. Then not yet 50 years old, Ferrari has since enslaved the minds of many who willingly dedicate every leisure hour to advance the legend. No other car maker can frustrate and satisfy at the same time, a fact well illustrated should one try to obtain information from Modena. When he was alive Il Commendatore was rarely satisfied; always he looked for something better. He and his company never stood still, never rested on the laurels of past accomplishments.

Even before the 400 was dead and the birth of the 500 Superfast took place, the 330 America began production.

Really a stop-gap model, the 330 America was the 250 GTE 2+2 with a new engine design based upon the 400 Superamerica. Improvements to this engine included lengthening the distance between the cylinder bore centers for better water circulation. Horsepower was rated at 300 bhp at 6,600 rpm, but historians wink knowingly and add a further 40 horses.

Once again the engine was based on Colombo's design; but who did what to make it more efficient is open to conjecture. After Colombo and Lampredi had gone, Ferrari was loath to identify engineers even though he had great men at his elbow. Vittorio Jano, one time Alfa Romeo racing-engine designer, for one; Franco Roccri for another. And then there was the gifted Luigi Bazzi, a technician for whom little appeared impossible. So whatever was done was done by these and others who one day will achieve the recognition they justly deserve.

Fifty 330 Americas née 250 GTEs were built before the "proper" 330 GT 2+2 was introduced at the January 1964 Ferrari press conference. Many guests were surprised; had the great Enzo relinquished his dynamism? For what they saw on stage was a two-door family coupé with four headlamps and lackluster styling by Pininfarina; lackluster by the standards of Ferrari enthusiasts. Apart from the traditional Borrani wire wheels (later to be replaced by cast alloy wheels as standard) and the Prancing Horse, the 330 could have been the result of some other manufacturer's dream.

Between 1964 and 1967, 1,080 330 2+2s were built, a high number indeed for a Ferrari. For many years this car has languished at the bottom of the Ferrari list – the present author ruefully recalls that he turned down a very respectable 330 GT 2+2 offered at around $4,500. The year was 1983. Now look what they are worth ....

By 1965 the four-headlight-look reminiscent of a dragonfly was deleted in favor of twin beams. Apparently there was an outcry over the quads, with many an angry enthusiast imploring the normally intractable concern to revise the 330. To give Ferrari credit, he or his company listened, and the subsequent twin headlight version was a great improvement.

Quite clearly Pininfarina was Ferrari's favorite stylist and it could be said that much of his fame came from the Ferraris he and his son Sergio and son-in-law Renzo Carli were to produce. The 500 Superfast (previous pages and right) took over where the 400 Superamerica left off. The tail fins of ten years before had gone and in their place a sensual sloping tail style which was to characterize the Superfast series. The model was introduced at the 1965 Geneva Motor Show. The engine designed for the car was of 5 liter capacity producing 400 bhp at 6,500 rpm, making it one of the most powerful road cars of the period.

SPECIFICATIONS
500 Superfast Series 1&2

Type	500
Model	SF Superfast
Years made	1964-1966
Chassis range	5951-8897
Number produced	37
Coachbuilders	Pinin Farina
Body styles	Coupé
Body material	Steel
Seating capacity	2
Engine type	V12 60°
Displacement	4961cc
Bore and stroke	88mm x 68mm
Cyl. head	SOHC, single outside plug
Ignition	2 distributors
Compression	8.8 and 9.0 to 1
Carburation	3 x 40DCZ/6
Lubrication	Wet sump
Horsepower	400bhp @ 6500rpm
Chassis/Drivetrain	Engine/gearbox in front
Frame	Tubular – maintubes elliptical
Transmission	S1 4-speed + overdrive /S2, 5-speed
Axle ratio	Various
Brakes	Hydraulic discs
Wheels	15" Borrani wire
Front suspension	Independent, A-arms, coil springs, telescopic shocks
Rear suspension	Live axle, semi elliptical springs, telescopic shocks
Curb weight	3400lbs
Wheelbase	2650mm
Track front	1397mm
Track rear	1389mm

A car of far greater significance than the 330 GT first appeared at the 1964 Paris Salon. Introduced at a time when the exclamations over the last Modena creation had died down, the 275 GTB more than made up for the unfortunate 330 GT. It was as inspired as the GTO, as stylish as the California and so beautiful that few cars since have been able to equal the design by Pininfarina at his company's best. Due to the enormous pressure involved designing and building other Ferraris as well as working with other car makers, Pininfarina was relieved by Scaglietti, who built the 275 GTB during its four years of production.

Underneath the series of sensuous, rounded curves that was the 275 GTB's body lay a distinct departure from the traditional Ferrari norm. There was nothing special about the V12 engine; this was pure Colombo at 3.3 liters and could develop 280 bhp when fitted with 3 Weber carburetors, 300 bhp if equipped with the optional 6 Webers. What was different was the suspension. For the first time on a production road car Ferrari employed independent suspension all round. Brakes were hydraulic discs and the transmission a five-speed transaxle. Borrani wire wheels were relegated to the small Ferrari option list; attractive

Right: the Pininfarina-bodied 500 Superfast was in the range for two years and came in two series. There swere 25 Series 1 cars and 12 Series 2 cars. The Series 2 models had a five-speed gearbox. The 500 Superfast was the ultimate luxury Ferrari and this was reflected in the customer list, which included such individuals as Prince Aga Khan, Prince Bernhard of the Netherlands, the Shah of Iran and actor Peter Sellers.

Compagnolo alloys were standard.

While the body of the 275 GTB was as fine a piece of road-going sculpture as any yet devised, the car was not without its problems. On the earlier GTBs the driveshaft was supported by a central bearing and had solid couplings at either end. This gave rise to considerable alignment problems, and even when the couplings were replaced with constant velocity joints, this malady, though eased, was never entirely corrected during the life of the car.

Displayed at the Paris Salon at the same time as the GTB was the 275 GTS Spyder. Its underpinnings were almost identical to the 275 GTB, with the result it had much the same problems. For some reason the 3.3-liter engine was detuned to 260 bhp in the GTS and while the Pininfarina-designed and built body was practical, it was inferior to the GTB from a looks standpoint.

Four hundred and sixty of the first GTB were assembled, and when the second series was introduced in late 1965 it was immediately obvious that there were differences. The nose was longer, the grille slightly smaller – and then there was the hood bulge ....

That bulge hid another first for a street Ferrari. Its designation was now GTB/4, which told the world that the bulge covered twin cams on each cylinder bank, four in all. Based again on Colombo's V12, this engine developed 300 bhp in standard trim and was capable of hurtling the 275/4 to an awesome 155-160 mph. When production came to an end in 1968, 350 of the 4 cam long nose GTBs had been built.

Ferrari also built eleven coupés for competition and these were referred to as 275 GTB/C models. Dry sump lubrication was used, as were strengthened camshafts, special carburetors, crankshaft and valves. A further nine extremely special Cabriolets were built at the request of Luigi Chinetti, Jr, son of Ferrari's major US distributor. These were called NART Spyders after Chinetti's North American Racing Team and are priceless cars today.

One of the most impressive sports cars ever built, the 275 GTB/4 had everything Ferrari is famous for. Though only a two-seater its interior was comfortable and well thought out, proving the point that Ferrari was extremely serious about his road-going cars. Listen to the infectious melody of those 12 cylinders breathing life into every corner of this beautifully constructed machine. Depress the clutch, move the wonderfully smooth stick into first, note the harmony as the engine takes up the slack. One will know why Ferraristis are so enthusiastic. One will have seen, felt, become part of the mystique.

B-GTB and A-GTB. Before GTB and after GTB. Maybe that is how the history books will one day tell the Ferrari story to our great great grandchildren. Certainly in 1968 the GTB/4 was difficult to emulate, and while few Ferraris since have been able to compare – in stylistic terms, at least – a lot of admittedly interesting models have left their mark. There was the 330 GTS Pininfarina convertible; a hundred of these were made between 1966 and 1968. Then came the nearest thing to the artistry of the 275 GTB. Shown for the first time at Ferrari's familiar stamping ground, the Paris Salon, the 1968 365 GTB/4 Daytona certainly roused the motoring press.

Another Pininfarina design, another model built by Scaglietti, the 365 GTB/4 Daytona was handsome indeed. Christened Daytona by the press, the GTB/4 was the most expensive and fastest Ferrari ever offered as a road car. Not only the quickest Ferrari but with a 174 mph plus top speed, it was the fastest production car made up to that time. Its 4.4-liter DOHC V12 developed a vital 352 bhp at 7,500 rpm, but competition versions produced an even greater 450 horsepower in 1973.

SPECIFICATIONS
Dino 206S Prototype Sports Mid Engine

65° 1986cc, 86 x 57mm, 218 bhp at 9000 rpm, CR 10.8:1, double ohc per bank, single plug per cylinder, coil ignition, 3 40 DCN2 Webers, 5 speed gearbox, integral with final drive.

FS Ind double wishbones, coil springs
RS as FS
Wheelbase 2280mm
Track Front 1360mm Rear 1355mm

Notes: Introduced – through chassis 0842 – at Ferrari press conference February 1966. First seen in competition at **Sebring 12 Hour 26 March 1966** when it was driven by Lorenzo Bandini & Ludovico Scarfiotti and finished 1st in class and 5th overall. The intention was to make 50 of these cars for homologation as 2 litre Group 4 sports cars. Industrial unrest affected the competition side as well as the production cars and was allied to the problems of keeping going in Formula 1 and prototype sports racing. This meant that in the long run only 18 – chassis numbers 002-036 – were built. A number were fitted with Lucas fuel injection in place of Weber carburettors. Some had two plugs per cylinder and also available were heads with 18 valves. These variations seem to appear or disappear either singly, in various combinations or as a full package.
For complete chassis by chassis and race history of these cars, see **Ferrari Vol. 17 Nos. 3 & 4** – special issue of the journal of the American Ferrari Owners Club by Marcel Massini and Denny Schue.

From its steeply raked, deep windshield to its wind-splitting front end, the 365 GTB/4 was everything the man with a James Bond fixation would require. It was exceedingly fast, had brutish good looks, a stylish yet masculine two-seater interior and a personality that took some getting used to. In other words, it was a tough car to handle; the driver had to keep his wits about him 100 percent of the time.

Early versions had quad headlights set behind a flush-mounted, full-width wrap-around clear plastic cover. Because this and the headlight height did not meet US requirements this attractive and functional styling ploy gave way to hidden lights, which popped up at the flick of a switch. Many admirers thought the hidden lights looked better; certainly the US authorities did, thus allowing the Daytona into America from mid-1971. By now Ferrari was fully conversant with American needs and the Daytona could be ordered with air conditioning (which was not that good), leather seats and other refinements. American safety and environmental regulations had increased and became more insistent from 1968, so Ferrari had to comply if cars were to sell stateside.

In 1969 a convertible version, the 365 GTS/4 Daytona Spyder, was unveiled at the Frankfort Motor Show. Only available to special order, 123 were produced as compared to 1,300 Berlinettas. Of course, all the surviving Spyders have been eagerly snapped up by collectors and at present fetch a very high price. One should be aware, though, that there are many non-factory Spyders in existence. Chassis numbers will not distinguish a factory original from an aftermarket conversion, either. Unfortunately, Berlinetta and Spyder numbers ran consecutively from 12,037 to 17,087.

The Ferrari Dino 206P (previous and facing pages) was an out-and-out prototype racing car with a 2-liter V6 engine producing over 200 bhp. In its first form it was used by Grand Prix driver Ludovico Scarfiotti for the European 2-liter hill climb championship from July 1965 and destroyed the then-dominant Porsches. For the 1966 season Ferrari wanted to build 50 206Ps to qualify as a Group 4 2-liter sports car, but pressure in the racing department and industrial problems in the factory saw only a handful being made. The car photographed was one of these new cars, with bodywork designed by Piero Drogo.

A number of other 365 models followed the Daytona, such as the 1971 365 GTC/4. Supposedly a more civilized "unisex" version of the GTB/4 the GTC/4 had AMX Javelin-type front fenders and an awkward fastback roof-line. Mechanically similar to the GTB/4, the car was more refined, some say less exciting. Three hundred of these Pininfarina-designed and built GTC/4s were assembled before production ended in 1972.

Family luxury had actually started with the 330 GT 2+2 and continued in 1967 with the 365 GT 2+2. It was obvious with this Pininfarina coupé with its 4.4-liter front-engined V12 that Ferrari was beginning to recognize that two seats do not necessarily equate with luxury. This handsome car with styling not unlike the 500 Superfast, had an extra pair of rear seats that could accommodate taller passengers; Rolls-Royce and Cadillac take heed! Independent suspension was used for the first time on a Ferrari 2+2 and in the three years the car was produced, 800 examples were sold.

Announced in 1972 and production ending in 1976, the 365 GT4/2+2 GT was actually a GTC/4 but with two additional seats. With its refined behavior the GT4/2+2 was Ferrari at the country club, Ferrari at a dinner/dance, Ferrari at the theater. A family Ferrari with enough power under the hood to shake off any would-be traffic-light grand prix racer. About 470 were made.

Then in 1976 Ferrari really appeared to be showing its middle-aged maturity with the announcement of the 400

From the rear, the Piero Drogo 206P racer (right) displayed the latest concepts in aerodynamic design but retained the brutal starkness of a racing car. As so few were built Ferrari could not homologate it for the production class so it ran as a prototype in the 1966 season.

GT, equipped with GM's Turbo-hydramatic automatic transmission as standard. The car itself was a large, conventional, razor-edged family coupé – at least Ferrari resisted the temptation for four doors!

The 400 GT 2+2 was an outstanding luxury automobile. Finish was high compared to normal Italian standards of workmanship, though Rolls-Royce and Lincoln were still superior in this field.

After 500 of the carburetted 5-liter 400 GT 2+2 had been built, they were followed by the 400i, the "i" indicating that the new model was fuel injected.

Bosch worked closely with Ferrari on a suitable fuel-injection system for the big V12, which, after many years of production and modifications, was still ahead of most of the opposition.

From 294.3 cid (4823 cc) to 300 (4943 cc) emerged the Bosch K- Jetronic fuel-injected V12 in Ferrari's latest – and so far best – luxury car. Introduced in 1985 the 412 2+2 is still with us. Developing 340 bhp at 6,000 rpm, the sleek notchback car certainly holds its own in luxury with its sumptuously appointed and very refined interior. As sleek and refined as it is, however, the 412 does not possess the Ferrari magic. There is little to distinguish it from the many other luxury cars competing for custom.

Fortunately the above comment does not hold true for the many other Ferrari models that have crossed the world's motoring stage these past twenty-five years. New powerplants entered the arena along with cars that were as good as their contemporaries yet better than most. Of the engines, the flat twelve was quite a departure from tradition – and so was the V8.

Not seriously used in Formula 1 competition until 1971, the Flat 12 engine had its first outing as early as 1964 when a 1.5-liter unit was driven in the Monza GP time trials, though it did not actually race until the US Grand Prix. Although it performed well throughout the 1965 season, the flat 12 did not win a Grand Prix.

Ferrari had captured the prestigious European Hill Climb Championship on two separate occasions in the past, but lost to Porsche who dominated the event until 1969. Using a 2-liter (121.5 cid) flat 12 designed by engineer Jacoponi for the sole purpose of wresting the championship back from the Germans, Ferrari did just that. Developing over 315 bhp at 11,800 rpm – it is a wonder the engine did not fly apart – the 48-valve flat 12, 212 E (for Europa) Montagna left the Porsches in puzzled disarray to win by a convincing margin.

For the 1971 Grand Prix season Ferrari yielded a 182.5 cid – or 3 liter – flat 12 called the 312 PB (Prototypo Boxer – incidentally Boxer is a German nickname for the horizontally opposed configuration applied to Ferrari's and other "flat" engines). This engine produced 440 bhp at 10,800 rpm in a body that weighed little more than 1,290 pounds. As already noted, the engine is horizontally opposed, the cylinder banks set at a 180 degree angle from each other. Of course, there were twin overhead camshafts for each cylinder bank. Lucas fuel injection and a five-speed gearbox were positioned behind the mid-mounted engine.

Fast and furious Ferrari drivers drove the 312 PBs, and while they led in every race, breakdowns and crashes prevented any wins until 1972, when the flat 12s finally captured the Championship.

Whatever Ferrari does it does well. It gets hold of an idea and perfects it. But Ferrari has never really been innovative. Take the flat 12 for instance. Chevrolet used that configuration in its much maligned Corvair, and Porsche were winning races with its flat 12 long before Ferrari. As Ferrari's engineers perfected the pair of V12s so too did they

improve and develop the Flat 12 into the marvelous engine it is today.

Ferrari has to put up with Maserati and Lamborghini in close proximity to his Modena factory. By the early 'seventies both had advanced rear-engined cars on sale to the public. At this time, the traditional front engine, rear-drive Daytona was Ferrari's flagship, until 1973 when Ferrari put into production the Pininfarina-designed 365 GT4 BB.

First shown at Turin in 1972, the 365 GT4 BB (Berlinetta Boxer) had a 4.4-liter (300.8 cid) flat-12 set amidships, directly behind the none too roomy two-place cockpit. Transmission was a five-speed all-synchromanual and the suspension was all-independent with unequal A-arms, coil springs and telescopic shock absorbers.

Pininfarina's styling was completely different from the Daytona. Rounded, aerodynamic body lines gave way to a low slung, flat front end with more overhang than at the rear. In fact, the overhang was so dramatic that the prominently curved fender wells are only inches ahead of the windshield's A-pillars.

Previous page: the 250 GT Lusso was followed by the 275 GTB and in turn this led, at the Paris Motor Show of 1966, to the 275 GTB/4. The final figure 4 was added as with this model the four-cam cylinder head was used. A similar design had been used in the racing cars at least fifteen years before. Designed by Pininfarina, this side view illustrates the steady evolution of Pininfarina's design themes. Facing page: this dramatic overhead picture of the car again underlines the overall symmetry of the Pininfarina design. The glass area has been increased and the front end smoothed off and rounded. The car was built locally in Modena by Scaglietti, the chassis being delivered by transporter from Maranello.

SPECIFICATIONS
275GTB/4

Type	275
Model	GTB/4
Years made	1966-1968
Chassis range	8769-11069
Number produced	350
Coachbuilders	Scaglietti
Body styles	Berlinetta
Body material	Steel or aluminum
Seating capacity	2
Engine type	V12 60°
Displacement	3285cc
Bore and stroke	77mm x 58.8mm
Cyl. head	DOHC, single outside plug
Ignition	2 distributors
Compression	9.2 to 1
Carburation	6 x 40DCN17
Lubrication	Dry sump
Horsepower	300bhp @ 8000rpm
Chassis/Drivetrain	Engine front/gearbox rear
Frame	Tubular steel – maintubes oval
Transmission	5-speed transaxle
Axle ratio	3.55 to 1
Brakes	Hydraulic discs
Wheels	14" cast alloy
Front suspension	Independent, A-arms, coil springs, telescopic shocks
Rear suspension	Independent, A-arms, coil springs, telescopic shocks
Curb weight	2750lbs
Wheelbase	2400mm
Track front	1401mm
Track rear	1417mm

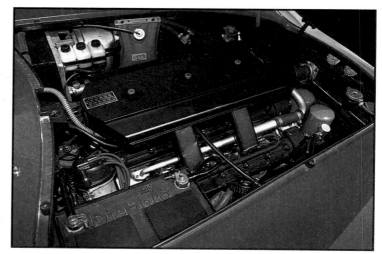

Above and right: the 275 GTB/4 used a 3.3-liter engine producing just under 300 bhp. It was an extremely quick car, the French racing driver Jean Pierre Beltoise covering 46 miles in under 23 minutes including stopping at a French motorway toll booth! This was before universal speed limits, but underlined that despite the fact the 275 GTB/4 was a road car it was blessed with an incredible performance potential. As can be seen in the rear view (facing page), an aerodynamic rear spoiler helped to improve the handling. The slight bulge on the bonnet identifies the 275 GTB/4 as against the smooth bonnet of the 275 GTB The cockpit design followed the traditional style, with pale warm leather bucket seats and five-speed gearbox operated through a chrome-faced slotted change.

To get at the engine the whole back end lifts rearward to reveal the complete unit and rear suspension besides. The rear view might have been a little restricted by the narrow, upright back window.

In 1976, after 387 BBs had been built by Scaglietti, the Paris Motor Show saw a modified version take over from the 365. This was the 512 BB, which looked almost exactly the same as the 365 BB, the only differences being four tail-lights instead of six and air intakes ahead of the rear wheels. What major differences there were, were in the engine, which was tweaked to 301.6 cid (4942 cc). This was thought to have been done to help meet increasing emissions restrictions enacted by the U.S. and some European countries. It did not help because Ferrari was not successful in meeting stringent US standards and it was left to American specialist shops to modify BBs that entered the country.

In mid-1981 the 512 BB became the 512 BBi engine with the fitting of Bosch K-Jetronic fuel injection instead of the previous carburetors. Horsepower remained 340 as did top speed of around 160 mph (*Road & Track* clocked a 512 at 168 mph).

Of the 512 BB, 929 were built and a further 1,007 fuel injected versions were produced before the car was phased out in 1984. Then, in the autumn of 1984, visitors to the annual Paris Salon saw the unveiling of the long-awaited BB replacement. The Testarossa had arrived.

Nothing remotely like its namesake, the 1985 Testarossa was Ferrari's new flagship. Its flamboyant Pininfarina-styled body was obviously meant to compete with the excessively vulgar Lamborghini Countach. One would have hoped Ferrari was above Lamborghini's tasteless exuberance, but times have changed. Fiat owns Ferrari completely and big corporations like Fiat think lire first. Brash youngsters and men who think they are Donald Trump buy eye-catching vulgarity. If Lamborghini can do it and survive then so can Ferrari.

In the author's opinion the Testarossa is vulgar. It is also rather ostentatious, with little about its styling that appeals to the sensitive eye. But there are areas that are attractive, such as the controversial side grilles with their razor-sharp edges that flow from the front of the doors to the fenders. This piece of styling is beautifully executed and serves an additional purpose; that of directing air into the cleverly positioned radiators set either side, just ahead of the rear wheels. This placement of the radiators was dictated by better weight distribution and a trifle more available space.

The flat-12 engine is the same as in the old Boxer (so is much of the rest of the Testarossa) but it differs inasmuch as it has adopted 4 valves per cylinder head. Horsepower is 390 in Europe, 380 in the US. What is really impressive is the car's width. It is so wide that even a Cadillac looks starved by comparison.

Inside the car space is relative. By that I mean it is great if one measures 4 feet nothing, but a Harlem Globetrotter might be better off with an old Checker limousine. The Testarossa is not that roomy but there are worse. As a driver, though, one begins to realize what one is paying for; it is true state of the art technology. Admittedly the narrow seats might not help ones disposition, but once crammed in, the car is absolute perfection to drive.

So far Ferrari has built over 2,000 Testarossas and there appear to be a few more years left for it. Designed to meet America's stringent emissions and safety standards, it has helped Ferrari profits immeasurably. The "Redhead" (Testarossa) is a fine car – yet it does not have the class of its forebear.

Before looking at the V8s and the extraordinary F-40

SPECIFICATIONS
365 California GT

4390cc, 81 x 71mm, 320 bhp at 6600 rpm, CR 8.8:1, single ohc per bank, single plug per cylinder, coil ignition, 3 Webers, 5 speed gearbox integral with engine.

FS Ind double wishbones, coil springs
RS Rigid axle, semi elliptic springs
Wheelbase 2650mm
Track Front 1405mm Rear 1397mm

Notes: Introduced Geneva Show, Spring 1966. Considered by some to be the last of the large engined luxury cars as typified by the **375 America, 410 and 400 Superamerica** and **500 Superfast.** It was the only one to go into production as a spyder. Bodies designed and built by Pinin Farina. Production which lasted through to mid 1967 was very limited, only 14 examples in a chassis number range 8347 to 10369

there is a very special range of cars built by Ferrari yet not Ferraris in name. They were called Dino ....

Alfredo "Dino" Ferrari died very young. He should have been able to enjoy the flower of his youth, yet the good things of early life were denied him when he contracted the disease of muscular dystrophy. Often bed ridden during his short life, Dino had taken a great interest in his famous father, Enzo Ferrari's affairs. And so it was that his father's great friend Vittorio Jano and Ferrari had discussed the possibility of a V6 engine with Dino, whose knowledge of engineering matters was exceptional. Even though ill, Dino had acquired an engineering degree and had written articles discussing the feasibility of a V6 engine.

Up to this point Enzo had never considered a V6 format, but long hours at his son's bedside, with Vittorio Jano also present, finally convinced him that Dino was right.

Shortly after, Dino passed away leaving his grief-stricken father determined to honor his son in whatever way he could. Already work was almost complete on the first V6, a Vittorio Jano/Dino Ferrari design, to be used in Formula 2 racing. Five months after Dino's death the 1.5-liter DOHC V6 with twin ignition and developing 175 bhp at 8,300 rpm, was born. It was naturally called the Dino 156 F2.

As good as the engine was, Ferrari felt it too complicated for private entrants, so Jano designed a SOHV V6 instead. This was the 1965 which went racing in 1959, with dismal results. Then came the larger 2065 engine (by the way, 2065 means two liter six) in 1960 with equally miserable results. Undeterred, Ferrari's next try was with the 2.5 liter 2465. This was the last front-engine Dino to be built and was not much more successful than the previous cars (it managed a 4th place in the 1960 Targa Florio). Returning to the drawing board, work on a mid-engine design of Mauro Forghieri and Franco Rocchi, brilliant engineers both, resulted in the third generation V6 which was good enough for serious production. It was a 65-degree four-cam unit displacing 147 ci (2417 cc) and rated at 270 bhp at 8,000 rpm. First shown at a Ferrari press conference in February 1961, the engine saw service in a Dino 246 SP Prototype Sports racing car. Two were built and did reasonably well in their racing adventures. Their best was a win at the 1961 Targa Florio and a third place at Nurburgring.

In 1962, two V6 Dinos were shown: the 196 SP and 286 SP (SP means Prototype Sports) – only the 196 SP raced and performed satisfactorily throughout the season.

Previous and facing pages: the 365 California roadster was introduced at the 1966 Geneva Motor Show, but despite the fact that it carried the California name it was aimed at a specific market; the same upper class market at which the 500 Superfast was directed.

The 365 California (these pages) introduced a number of new styling ideas, including an air intake along the door and into the leading edge of the rear wing (second top). This idea was to appear in other designs for the next twenty years, but was both novel and futuristic in 1967. Another design innovation was a sculpted tail with a specially shaped rear light cluster to match the shape (left). For this model Pininfarina returned to the binnacle design for the main instruments and dials on the dashboard. The standard of finish matched the aspirations of the small number of well-heeled buyers who were able to buy 365 Californias. According to Ferrari records only 14 were built.

If not the most successful, certainly the most glamorous of the Dino racers was the 1966 206 SP. As can be seen from the photographs, this was an inspired piece of automotive sculpture, hence the reason this is one of very few competition cars included in this book.

Powered by a 2.0-liter version of Forghieri and Rocchi's V6, it was intended to build fifty examples for homologation as 2-liter Group 4 sports cars. Due to industrial unrest and Ferrari's interest in Formula One racing, only eighteen – chassis numbers 002-036 – were actually built. However, as sports racing cars go, this mid-engined 206 SP is a work of pure art. Dudley Mason-Styrron, who has owned the illustrated car for a number of years, regularly fields it in competition across Europe and England, and says it is a wonderful driving machine which has chalked up several successes in recent years. Its engine develops 218 bhp at 9,000 rpm and is the usual 65-degree unit with dual overhead camshafts. The body design was the work of Piero Drogo's body shop and is probably his finest work to date.

Previous pages: another Ferrari 275 GTB/4, of which only around 280 were built. The production run of the car was curtailed after eighteen months due to American Federal Safety Regulations. This concerned emission controls which would have greatly reduced the power and efficiency of the 3.3-liter engine. It did, however, hasten the design of their next car, which was to become another classic: the Daytona. Above left: the chrome Borrani wheels, which had become something of a trademark on Ferraris, were to change after the GTB/4. This model brought to an end a certain era for the gran turismo Ferraris, their whole shape and character changing into what today we would call the modern Ferraris.

1972 FERRARI 365 GTB/4 DAYTONA

Dino 206 SPs notwithstanding, a beautiful production model, the 206 GT, appeared in 1967. It came with all the accouterments necessary of a modern sports car, including a 5-speed transaxle, all independent suspension and a V6 2.0-liter (121.3 cid) engine placed transversely behind the two-seat passenger compartment. Two prototypes shown earlier had the engine situated in the longitudinal position, but it was agreed the sideways mounting was much better.

One hundred and fifty of these all-aluminum bodied 206 GTs were built by the end of 1969 – production had only begun at the beginning of the year – when the exciting and lovely Dino 246 GT was announced. Engine displacement went up to 2.4 liters and horsepower to 195. American versions were at 180 bhp and all engines now had a cast-iron block instead of aluminum as before. All-steel bodies replaced the earlier aluminum 206 GT models.

All told there were three versions of this highly successful model, which was the least expensive car Ferrari had ever put into production. Starting in 1969 the series ended in 1974, but not before a Dino GTS (Spyder) had been put into production in 1971. Of Type L on the first series 357 were produced, followed by 507 Type M/Series II and then Type E, which included the 246 GTS, continued until 1974, making a grand total of 3,883 Dino 246 GTs and GTSs built. Without doubt one of the prettiest automobiles ever to come from Modena, the Dino was also one of the most successful. It goes without saying that Enzo Ferrari not only honored his son – he made his name a legend as well.

Before discussing the V8-engined Ferraris it is worth mentioning the Fiat Dino sports cars. Fiat and Ferrari had been moving closer together ever since Il Commendatore turned down Ford's take-over bid. By 1969 Fiat had complete control over Ferrari's affairs even while allowing his company complete independence in deciding what sort of cars to build.

A direct result of Fiat and Ferrari's earlier cooperation was the Fiat Dino. Two body styles, a 2+2 fastback designed by Bertone and a smart 1966. Both models used the Forghieri/Rocchi 2.0-liter V6 mounted at the front. Suspension was very conventional with independent front and a live axle at the rear.

In 1969 independent rear suspension was substituted in place of the live axle and the larger 2.4-liter engine replaced the 2.0-liter unit. Fiat assembled the engines and cars until almost the end of the run, when Ferrari took over engine assembly. Because Fiat's methods were geared to mass production, Ferrari was able to homologate his V6 as a Formula 2 production engine, a definite bonus for Modena. Of all Fiat Dino models, 7,651 were produced, a colossal number had Ferrari built them, but a very small figure for a giant like Fiat.

It is no stretch of the imagination to realize Ferrari's passion for multi-cylindered engines. Of course, 12 cylinders were his trademark and still are, even though he has experimented with four and six-cylinder configurations. But not eight. Apart from the odd company here and there,

SPECIFICATIONS
365GTB/4 'Daytona'

Type	365
Model	GTB/4 'Daytona'
Years made	1968-1973
Chassis range	12037-17087
Number produced	1300
Coachbuilders	Scaglietti
Body styles	Berlinetta
Body material	Steel
Seating capacity	2
Engine type	V12 60°
Displacement	4390cc
Bore and stroke	81mm x 71mm
Cyl. head	DOHC, single outside plug
Ignition	2 distributors
Compression	9.3 to 1
Carburation	6 x 40DCN20
Lubrication	Dry sump
Horsepower	352bhp @ 7500rpm
Chassis/Drivetrain	Engine front/transaxle rear
Frame	Tubular steel – maintubes oval
Transmission	5-speed transaxle
Axle ratio	3.3 to 1
Brakes	Hydraulic discs
Wheels	15" cast alloy
Front suspension	Independent, A-arms, coil springs, telescopic shocks
Rear suspension	Independent, A-arms, coil springs, telescopic shocks
Curb weight	3150lbs
Wheelbase	2400mm
Track front	1440mm
Track rear	1425mm

Note: Air conditioning was optional in Europe, and standard on all U.S. spec. cars.

In 1969, with competition from Lamborghini and others, Ferrari turned a new page with a car that essentially was a development of the GTB/4 but fitted with a bigger engine to try to overcome the emission problem. When it came to naming the new car Ferrari remembered his team's 1-2-3 victory in the Daytona race and so called the car "Daytona" (these and previous pages). The side view of the car again displays the sheer artistry of the Pininfarina design team, with a perfectly balanced shape for a front-engined car. It was introduced in 1968, the Paris Show once again being the showcase, but it did not go into production until the following year.

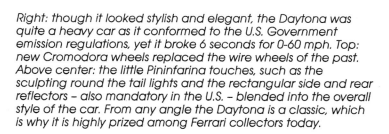

Right: though it looked stylish and elegant, the Daytona was quite a heavy car as it conformed to the U.S. Government emission regulations, yet it broke 6 seconds for 0-60 mph. Top: new Cromodora wheels replaced the wire wheels of the past. Above center: the little Pininfarina touches, such as the sculpting round the tail lights and the rectangular side and rear reflectors – also mandatory in the U.S. – blended into the overall style of the car. From any angle the Daytona is a classic, which is why it is highly prized among Ferrari collectors today.

eight cylinders appeared to be an American birthright. In the early 'sixties Ferrari became interested in eight-cylinders and the Dino, 248 SP came about. The solitary car had a 90-degree, 250-bhp V8 and only raced once before it was dropped, in 1962.

Eleven years were to pass before the V8 rose again, this time to power a new production 2+2 model. Shown at Paris in 1973 the Dino 308 GT 2+2 was the 246 GT replacement but powered by a 90-degree, 3-liter V8 putting out 250 horsepower. It was obvious Ferrari had produced a well-packaged design capable of hauling four passengers, and with V8 power it would be more than acceptable in many overseas markets, hence the specifications.

The Ferrari 365 GTS/4 (these and previous pages) was the official title for the car which everyone recognizes as the Daytona Spyder, and it was a logical development of the Daytona, retaining the pop-up headlights and sumptuous interior (above).

SPECIFICATIONS
365GTB/4-GTS/4 'Daytona Spyder'

Type	365
Model	GTB/4 GTS/4 'Daytona Spyder'
Years made	1969-1973
Chassis range	12851-17073
Number produced	123
Coachbuilders	Scaglietti
Body styles	Convertible
Body material	Steel
Seating capacity	2
Engine type	V12 60°
Displacement	4390cc
Bore and stroke	81mm x 71mm
Cyl. head	DOHC, single outside plug
Ignition	2 distributors
Compression	9.3 to 1
Carburation	6 x 40DCN20
Lubrication	Dry sump
Horsepower	352bhp @ 7500rpm
Chassis/Drivetrain	Engine front/transaxle rear
Frame	Tubular steel – maintubes oval
Transmission	5-speed transaxle
Axle ratio	3.3 to 1
Brakes	Hydraulic discs
Wheels	15" cast alloy
Front suspension	Independent, A-arms, coil springs, telescopic shocks
Rear suspension	Independent, A-arms, coil springs, telescopic shocks
Curb weight	3150lbs
Wheelbase	2400mm
Track front	1440mm
Track rear	1425mm

SPECIFICATIONS
246GTS

Type	246
Model	GTS
Years made	1972-1974
Chassis range	03408-08518
Number produced	1274
Coachbuilders	Scaglietti
Body styles	Coupé*
Body material	Steel
Seating capacity	2
Engine type	V6 65°†
Displacement	2418cc
Bore and stroke	92.5mm x 60mm
Cyl. head	DOHC, single outside plug
Ignition	1 distributor/dinoplex
Compression	9.0 to 1
Carburation	3 x 40DCN F/7
Lubrication	Wet sump
Horsepower	195bhp @ 7600rpm†
Chassis/Drivetrain	Engine/transaxle in rear
Frame	Tubular steel – maintubes oval
Transmission	5-speed transaxle
Axle ratio	
Brakes	Hydraulic discs
Wheels	14" cast alloy bolt-on
Front suspension	Independent, A-arms, coil springs, telescopic shocks
Rear suspension	Independent, A-arms, coil springs, telescopic shocks
Curb weight	2700lbs
Wheelbase	2340mm
Track front	1425mm
Track rear	1430mm

*Removable 'Targa' style roof
†Cast iron block – U.S.A. 180bhp.
Note: First U.S.A. car was 03764

Styled by Bertone and built by Scaglietti, 2,826 308 GT4 2+2s were built from 1974 to 1980. It has the distinction of being one of Ferrari's ugliest cars – in fact, apart from the engine and the wheels there is nothing attractive about it. In 1976 it became a Ferrari; perhaps the father did not want to insult his son's name.

Perhaps to stunt the criticisms leveled against the 308 GT4, Ferrari introduced a stylish 2-seater in 1975. This was the 308 GTB 2-passenger Berlinetta. Styled by Pininfarina, the GTB was a complete vindication of what Ferrari stood for; the fact that Scaglietti was fully committed in order to build 2,897 of them up to 1980 is proof of that.

Then came the detuned 208 GT4. Bore was reduced from 3.18 to 2.63 inches to arrive at 121.5 cid or 2.0 liters. The reason for this "economical" Ferrari was that the Italian market had to contend with high taxes and costly fuel which made larger cars too expensive to run.

Between 1975 and 1985 there came the 208 GTB, 208 GTS, 208 Turbo and 208 GTS Turbo. All these cars were much the same, with a few exceptions. One was the dramatic horsepower increase for the Turbo 208 which entered the picture in 1981. It went from 155 to 220 bhp.

New cylinder heads with four valves per cylinder came with the 308 in 1982. Still fuel injected by Bosch's familiar K-Jetronic system, the 308 GTB QV, the QV stood for "quattrovalve", developed 240 bhp in Europe, 230 in the US. This model was one of several 308s that emerged between 1977 and 1982; the 308 GTS; 308 GTSi – this arrived in 1980 and was fuel injected and of course, the aforementioned 308 GTS QV. In eight years, 8,002 units were built of these three variations; quite a lot for the man

The 246 GTS (these and previous pages) was a later open-topped version of the Dino 246 which used a 2.4-liter V6 engine. The Dino 246 GTS was a very stylish car with direction lights and front hood slots being symmetrically placed to maintain the balance. Behind the seats, the rear window (below) was curved more for design than practicality.

Above and right: to find the origins of the Ferrari Dino as a road car we must go back to the Paris Motor Show of 1965, where a mock up appeared on the Pininfarina stand in the coachwork section. The original production car was the 206 (2-liter 6-cylinder), but for 1970 the engine was enlarged to 2.4 liters and the 246 was born. The V6 engine slotted neatly behind the seats making it a true mid-engined sports car. At the front of the car the familiar Ferrari badge with the prancing horse symbol which had been given to Enzo Ferrari by Count Baracca was replaced by the name Dino in script. The name was repeated on the rear panel but the prancing horse was also added. The shape of the rear panel is reminiscent of the Ferrari Daytona.

1979 FERRARI 512 BERLINETTA BOXER

SPECIFICATIONS
512BB

Type	512
Model	BB
Years made	1976-1981
Chassis range	19711-38001 (?)
Number produced	929
Coachbuilders	Scaglietti
Body styles	Coupé
Body material	Aluminum
Seating capacity	2
Engine type	Flat 12
Displacement	4924cc
Bore and stroke	82mm x 78mm
Cyl. head	DOHC, single outside plug
Ignition	2 distributors
Compression	9.2 to 1
Carburation	4 x 40IF3C
Lubrication	Dry sump
Horsepower	340bhp @ 6800rpm
Chassis/Drivetrain	Engine/transaxle in rear
Frame	Tubular steel – maintubes oval
Transmission	5-speed transaxle
Axle ratio	
Brakes	Hydraulic discs
Wheels	15" alloy knock-ons
Front suspension	Independent, A-arms, coil springs, telescopic shocks
Rear suspension	Independent, A-arms, coil springs, telescopic shocks
Curb weight	3800lbs
Wheelbase	2500mm
Track front	1500mm
Track rear	1563mm

Note: No U.S. version available

who would normally make only a dozen or so of any model.

In 1980 the car that was called the successor to the 308 GT4 came about. Utilizing a 3.5-inch longer wheelbase than the 308, the Mondial 8, although a Pininfarina design, still did not meet with popular approval. Maybe stretching the wheelbase to 104 inches to give passengers more room was a good idea, but it would seem Pininfarina and other Italian designers become lost when asked to style a practical vehicle.

Be that as it may, the Mondial 8 featured an all-luxury interior. A panel on the dash gave warning of various problems that might occur and it was the first Ferrari to include tilt steering.

Mondials use the same V8 as did the 308s and as the two were built side by side until 1985, model frequency followed much the same course. All had fuel injection and horsepower ratings of 255 (Mondial 8), 240 for the Mondial QV and Cabriolet. In 1986 a 270 bhp version was introduced, mainly to revive lackluster American enthusiasm. Fifty pounds less weight, a shorter wheelbase and compression ratio up from 8.8:1 to 9.8:1 plus enough standard features such as air conditioning, power steering, power brakes, remote control driver's mirror and other amenities. Not quite what the traditional Ferrari enthusiast would want; but today's trendy young owner is attracted by the gadgets that leave little occasion for personal involvement or skill.

With Ferrari having moved to a mid-engined design with the Dino, it was logical to use the same layout for a larger car. The problem was that the V12 engine was too long to be mounted behind the seats as the wheelbase would have to be lengthened accordingly. The answer was to use a development of the flat 12 grand prix engine with the transmission below and so the Berlinetta Boxer concept was born. As can be seen, it retained a similar overall shape to the Dino but at the same time had a character of its own.

Top: access to the flat 12 cylinder engine was made easier by the ability to raise the entire rear bodywork of the Boxer. The car first appeared in prototype form at the 1971 Turin Motor Show and went into production in 1973 as the Ferrari 365 GT/4 Berlinetta Boxer with a 4.4-liter engine, and it was not until 1977 that the 5-liter version, the 512 BB was introduced. The 5-liter was slightly detuned and produced 340 bhp compared to the earlier model's 360. The car incorporated Daytona-style wheels (above), and even the cockpit was modified, with more comfortable seats and air conditioning. Though designed as a street car, a number of Berlinetta Boxers were prepared for racing which necessitated a fundamental redesign of the body to give a long tail to improve roadholding and aerodynamics. They were raced at Le Mans up to the mid-1980s.

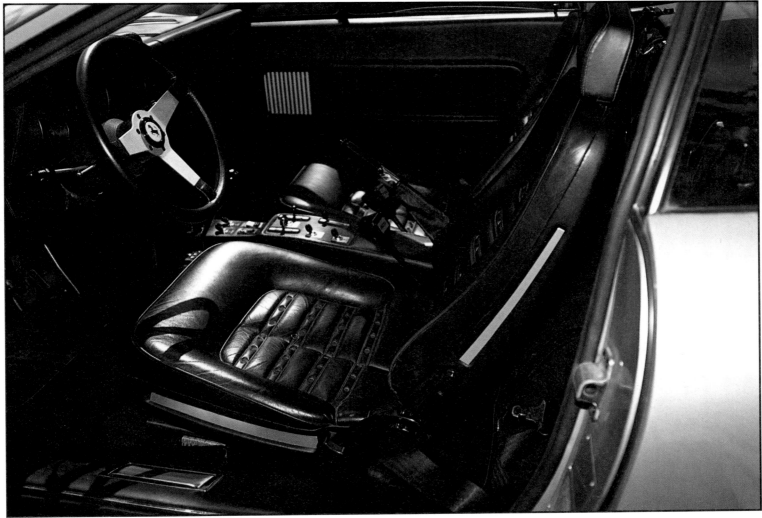

1984 FERRARI QUATTROVALVOLE 308

It would appear Pininfarina was rather uninspired when he first styled the 308 GTB. There is a look of the Dino 246 GT about it, though it is not quite as handsome. The same can be said for the 328 GTB/GTS announced in 1986. This also reminds one of the Dino but is squared off at the front, features hidden lights, rectangular sidelights set either side of the simple grille and black louvers where the C-pillar should be. Power is by the 3.2-liter V8, which is more than good enough for 150 mph.

When one talks of the GTO, 150 mph looks slow. Not the classic GTO, but the new one that came in 1984. Spoken of in respectful tones, figures such as 200 mph were heard. Well, the magic twin centuries were not achieved – 185 mph had to suffice, and notwithstanding what Lamborghini said, the Countach did not reach 200 mph either.

Announced on 22 February 1984 at Maranello, the 288 GTO was nothing if not an enigma. Its shape was nothing new – in fact, Pininfarina closely followed the lines of his earlier 308 GTB, although there was a very noticeable rear spoiler, triple slanted vents behind the rear wheels, Corvette style tail-lights and a large front spoiler. And those were about the only real differences on a car that supposedly only 200 would be made.

Of course the 288 GTO's engine was an enlarged version of the easy-going V8, though it was not as large as the 3185 cc unit driving the 328 and Mondial 3.2. In the GTO the engine barely touched 3 liters, not that this was all important. Horsepower was 400 and Scaglietti saved weight by fabricating most of the body panels from fiberglass, Kevlar, aluminum and Nomex.

That 200 were to be built meant Ferrari could homologate the GTO for Group B competition. Once that was achieved the plan was to build twenty racing versions. This never happened because the Group B class was suddenly discontinued. This did not bother buyers; the first 200 were sold sight unseen, before they were even made!

Production of the GTO ended in 1986 with 278 examples built. Factory price was a reported $76,000 – today the high end of six figures would be nearer. Actually, the GTO is hardly worth such a figure, for although its speed is phenomenal and it handles and drives well, it could not pass the European or US safety and emissions regulations. This meant that a buyer had to collect his order from the factory and then decide which loophole would enable him to get his purchase home: for Britain, all that was necessary was to register the GTO in its country of origin, in the owner's name. This way the car became a personal import, not one for resale.

Previous page: the Ferrari 308 Quatrovalvole (four valve) is the ultimate Dino, though by now the Dino badging had been dropped in favor of the normal Ferrari prancing horse. The original 308 GT4 had a Bertone-designed body, the first production body designed by anyone other than Pininfarina for 20 years. This original model was dropped in 1980. It was replaced by the 308 GTB which had been designed by Pininfarina and met with the approval of Ferrari enthusiasts who had shunned the Bertone design. The GTS Spyder range was introduced in 1978 with a "Targa" roof arrangement similar to the earlier Dinos, the center roof section being stored behind the seats when not in use. The engine was given a four valve cylinder head, leading to the "Quattrovalvole" name.

Above and right: the Quattrovalvole, the ultimate Dino, followed in the true Dino traditions by using a race-bred engine. The Dino engine traditionally had been looked upon as a V6, as it had been introduced in 1957 as a 1.5 liter Formula 2 engine and named after Enzo Ferrari's son Alfredino, but the 308 saw a street developed version of Ferrari's V8 grand prix engine used in a Dino chassis. The mandatory exhaust emission regulations in the United States called for drastic measures, as can be seen on the right with the complicated exhaust system on the 308 Quattrovalvole.

SPECIFICATIONS
Testarossa

Type	
Model	Testarossa
Years made	1985-
Chassis range	56,000(?)-
Number produced	1985, 568 & 1986, 819
Coachbuilders	Pinin Farina
Body styles	Coupé
Body material	Aluminum with steel
Seating capacity	2
Engine type	Flat 12
Displacement	4924cc
Bore and stroke	82mm x 78mm
Cyl. head	DOHC, 4 valves, single outside plug
Ignition	Digiplex
Compression	9.2 to 1
Carburation	Bosche K-Jetronic F.I.
Lubrication	Wet sump
Horsepower	390bhp* @ 6300rpm
Chassis/Drivetrain	Engine/transaxle in rear
Frame	Tubular, maintubes oval
Transmission	5-speed transaxle
Axle ratio	
Brakes	Hydraulic discs
Wheels	16" alloy knock-ons
Front suspension	Independent, A-arms
Rear suspension	Independent, A-arms
Curb weight	3660lbs
Wheelbase	2550mm
Track front	1518mm
Track rear	1660mm

*The U.S. version develops 380bhp

Another disadvantage was its lack of creature comfort. It had nothing. To the driver with sensitive hearing its noisiness sounded like the inside of a military tank. Then the finish left much to be desired. In one example which the author tried, both the inside and the outside paint was peeling off, and the leather-like material around the steering column was coming loose. A sad car, perhaps, because it was unable to realize its full potential when its class was dispensed with and Ferrari had spent much time developing the GTO for competition that never came.

With a full order book for as long as it is built, and priced at $210,000 each, and with the buyer collecting the car himself, the Ferrari F-40 would appear to have an assured future.

It is reputed to do 201 or more mph, this red machine of ducts and scoops, air dams and spoilers and the vertical rear stabilizers like cut down versions of the Superbird's from days gone by. The engine is in the middle, the same V8 as in the 288 but now 2936 cc instead of 2855 cc. Horsepower is a phenomenal 478 at 7,000 rpm and the engine sits under a clear plastic canopy punctured with air louvers, serving as a misty rear window that is of little use in the rain.

The Grand Old Man had requested a fortieth anniversary car to be put together, and the Ferrari Executive Committee (Ferrari, too has executive committees these days) had agreed. Thus the F-40 came into being: F-40 alludes to the fortieth anniversary.

It took just twelve months to develop the F-40, which probably was not difficult considering the extent to which it is based on the GTO. Underneath the low-slung body sitting on fat Pirelli tires there really is little new. No ABS brakes – 13-inch conventional hydraulic discs stop the car – no high-tech suspension, just the traditional A-arms, coils and telescopic shock absorbers.

Ferrari sells the F-40 for a massive $210,000, but quite often these cars sell for three times that within weeks. This situation is not to the liking of Ferrari, but there is little the company can do. One example the author saw in England was priced at one million pounds ($1,580,000), excessive by far. Especially when it is proposed to build 900 or more of the F-40.

Much of the F-40's undisguised race-car performance comes from the ill-fated GTO competition car. The only place a driver can achieve the F-40's full potential is, of course, on a race-track. To go beyond the speed limit in such a car would attract every policeman in the area. One would almost be tempted to show it in a static display in one's home.

On Sunday, 14 August 1988 Enzo Ferrari passed away, the last of the great motoring geniuses. His achievements in motor sport spanned sixty-eight years and his cars have all become legendary; they are the stuff healthy boys' dreams are made of. All over the globe men live and breathe Ferrari; its mystique has created an industry dabbling in everything from 1/43rd scale models, books and calendars to replicas.

To replace the Berlinetta Boxer, Enzo Ferrari came up with a car which stirred many happy memories for red-blooded Ferrari owners: the Testarossa (these and previous pages). This time there was no mistake made and Pininfarina were again entrusted with the body design. For this they came up with a body with a front end similar in side elevation to the Boxer's, but with a huge filigree-style air vent stretching along almost the full length of the door and into the rear wing. This was a practical solution to providing the rear radiators with plenty of air without contravening European laws. Seen from the rear (facing page top) the car seemed huge and it was certainly the widest Ferrari built, being six inches wider than a Berlinetta Boxer!

Regarding replicas, more and more are being discovered. Unscrupulous owners pass off reproductions of Testarossas, GTOs and Daytona Spyders as the genuine thing. With the advantages of modern technology, a talented forger can easily create a car difficult to distinguish from the real thing. If one should be in the position to buy a Ferrari, expert advice is essential to guide one's choice and prevent one being deceived.

Now that Il Commendatore has gone, what of the company he left behind? It is still intact and healthy, having behind it the enormous resources of Fiat. Other Ferraris are being planned at this moment and Modena intends to continue racing.

Information regarding the 348 replacement of the 328 is that it is a 170-mph V8-powered super car, with functional but luxurious interior; but its lack of riding comfort is disconcertingly noticeable when road ripples and undulations are met. It does not appear to have quite the magic of old.

Does this mean the 348 will become just another expensive sports-car? Or will the spirit of this enigmatic character named Enzo Ferrari continue to haunt the machines of Modena?

SPECIFICATIONS
F40

Type	
Model	F40
Years made	1988-
Chassis range	70167
Number produced	950 est.
Coachbuilders	Scaglietti
Body styles	Coupé
Body material	Kevlar and fibreglass
Seating capacity	2
Engine type	V8 90°
Displacement	2936cc
Bore and stroke	82mm x 69.5mm
Cyl. head	DOHC, 4 valves, single outside plug
Ignition	Weber Marelli
Compression	7.8 to 1
Carburation	Twin turbos + intercoolers
Lubrication	Dry sump
Horsepower	478bhp @ 7000rpm
Chassis/Drivetrain	Engine and gearbox in rear*
Frame	Tubular steel, Kevlar, carbon fibre and adhesive
Transmission	5-speed transaxle
Axle ratio	
Brakes	Hydraulic discs
Wheels	17" alloy forged
Front suspension	Independent, A-arms, coil springs, telescopic shocks
Rear suspension	Independent, A-arms, coil springs, telescopic shocks
Curb weight	2425lbs
Wheelbase	2450mm
Track front	1594mm
Track rear	1610mm

*Engine in longitudinal position

The Ferrari GTO of the 1980s was the precursor of the F40 (right and previous pages), Ferrari's latest and possibly ultimate expression of the GT style. Its design, looks and performance are as much a dream of the future turned into reality as many of the other Ferrari models. Powered by a twin turbocharged version of the 3-liter V8 engine it produces 478 bhp, the largest power output of any production Ferrari. The chassis is made of molded Kevlar and carbon fibre bonded to steel tubing.